Andrew D. White, Thornton Stringfellow, Andrew Dickson White

Slavery

Its origin, nature, and history: considered in the light of Bible teachings,

moral justice, and political wisdom.

Andrew D. White, Thornton Stringfellow, Andrew Dickson White

Slavery
Its origin, nature, and history: considered in the light of Bible teachings, moral justice, and political wisdom.

ISBN/EAN: 9783337412258

Printed in Europe, USA, Canada, Australia, Japan

Cover: Foto ©ninafisch / pixelio.de

More available books at **www.hansebooks.com**

ITS ORIGIN, NATURE, AND HISTORY,

CONSIDERED IN

THE LIGHT OF BIBLE TEACHINGS, MORAL JUSTICE, AND POLITICAL WISDOM.

LOVE the motto, not LIBERTY.

OBJECT.—Truth spoken in Love on the subject of Abolitionism. Its character freely, thoroughly to be discussed in the light of God's word, but with careful avoidance of personalities or ascription of motives. Hoping all things. Thinking no evil.

BY

REV. THORNTON STRINGFELLOW, D. D.,

OF CULPEPER COUNTY, VIRGINIA.

NEW YORK:
JOHN F. TROW, PRINTER, 50 GREENE ST.
1861.

EXTRACT FROM ADDRESS OF PROF. S. F. B. MORSE.

It cannot but be obvious to all intelligent minds, that among the complex questions which have so long agitated the whole land, and which have mingled their discordant elements in producing the present alarming political condition of the country, so deeply distressing to every patriotic mind, the moral and religious question of slavery stands forth most prominent. Indeed, it is the fundamental question, and demands, first of all, a satisfactory settlement; for on the right decision of this moral and religious question depend all the other questions relating to slavery. Whether slavery, or the condition of being held in subjection to the will of another, is a divine institution, sanctioned by laws and commands, and regulated from the earliest times, or is forbidden as a *sin*—as a violation of the laws of God—is surely a fundamental question. Difference here, at the start, is antipodal. The course of conduct pursued by the believers in these two extremes, must of necessity lead to results as diverse as light from darkness. Until this point is satisfactorily settled we cannot reach the expediency or inexpediency, the advantage or disadvantage, of this system of servitude. If it is a *sin*, if the Bible shows it to be a sin, the controversy is settled; we can have no compromise with sin; we have nothing to do with it but to forsake it. Hence all whose consciences sustain them in that view of the question are at least consistent in their zealous opposition to slavery, and their determination to uproot it everywhere and at all hazards. On the other hand, if God has shown in his word and by his providence, that servitude or slavery, in its various modifications of form and duration, and of mild or severe character, has, from the beginning of the world, been an essential feature in His government of man; that viewed from a loftier stand-point than is circumscribed by earth or time, there are benevolent ends in part comprehensible even by our short-sightedness, ends only attainable by this system, then they whose consciences sustain them in this view of the question, will be cautious how they rudely and recklessly fight against God and destroy it with violence. A glance at the character of the litigants on this question, show ranged on each side of the two opposing opinions, men of the highest intellectual and moral character. Rash, indeed, would it be to charge either party with hypocrisy. There is no need for such an uncharitable assumption. The humble seeker after truth will not suffer its golden sands to escape him, even if he has to separate them, with labor, from the mire of human weakness and error, and hence he may not neglect the extremest views of the bitterest opponents. Yet mindful of our own weakness and of our need of enlightenment, to what standard, but God's word, shall we appeal as the arbiter in such a controversy? "To the law and to the testimony."

SLAVERY AND GOVERNMENT.

CHAPTER I.

What Slavery is—What Freedom is—None are 'born' free: all are 'born' slaves—Slavery a necessity—Why the white race is invested with political freedom at twenty-one—Why it is withheld from the black race for life—Slavery is just, and why—None are born equal: inequality the ground of social happiness—What government is: what its object is: where it originated: by whom it should be exercised, and why—Inferiority of the black race: the proof of it.

It is not many years since our brethren at the North engaged in a crusade against Slavery; because (as they said) it was denounced in every page of the Bible as the greatest sin on earth.

The Bible has been examined, and it has been found that slavery is fully sanctioned by it. Nevertheless, this crusade has waxed warmer against slavery, as a sin of the deepest dye; because it was a sin (as they have said) against a higher law than the Bible. No appeal is now made to the Bible, but to consciences begotten by infidelity. By this new conscience every question of right and wrong is to be tried, and every penalty inflicted. These crusaders have adopted as their Bible, on the subject of slavery, Mr. Jefferson's declaration, that "all men are born free and equal." It may not be amiss then to try this new Bible by the common sense and the common observation of all men—to see whether it ought to have preference over the old Bible, before we throw the old one away, as our brethren of the North do when it conflicts with their new anti-slavery Bible. First, then, let us inquire,

What is Slavery in the United States?

Answer.—It is a system of personal servitude, under a form of government adopted for the African race, the leading principle of which belongs to every form of government among men.

Question.—What is that leading principle?

Answer.—It is submission to, and control by the will of another. This is the essential principle of all forms of government; and without it there can be no government. It is the principle ordained of God for the government of a family. Its administration is given of God to the heads of families, who have instinctively accepted and acted upon it in all ages and countries.

Question.—What is the amount of power in their hands to enforce obedience over children and slaves? And what is the object aimed at in its exercise?

Answer.—The amount of power in their hands to enforce obedience over children and slaves, is limited to the use of all *necessary* and *proper* means to secure obedience, and the object aimed at in its exercise, is to develop their faculties, and fit them to take care of families, and discharge political duties.

Question.—What is a slave in the United States?

Answer.—A slave, according to the Federal Constitution, is a person who owes service or labor to another person. In the language of the Scriptures, he is a "man's money."

Question.—What is an apprentice in the United States?

Answer.—An apprentice according to the Constitution, is a person who owes service or labor to another person.

Question.—Does a child stand in the same relation to his father, (as regards service and subjection to his will,) that an apprentice or slave does to his master?

Answer.—Yes, until he is twenty-one years old.

Question.—Is this service, or labor of children, apprentices, and slaves, legal property in the United States?

Answer.—Yes, it is so declared by the laws of every State in the Union, except as to slaves, and by the slaveholding States as to them.

Question.—What is the difference, then, between a slave and a white minor who is called free?

Answer.—The difference is that a slave of the black race owes labor and subjection to his master for life; while the white minor and apprentice only owe service and subjection until they are twenty-one years old.

Question.—Has a parent a legal property right in the service or labor of his child, and a legal right to control him and coerce him to obedience without his consent?

Answer.—Yes, he has exactly the same property right in the service or labor of his child until he is twenty-one years old, and exactly the same right to control him, and to coerce obedience to his authority until that time, that the master has in and over his slave.

Question.—Has the parent of the child, and the master of the slave, unlimited discretion in compelling obedience to their authority?

Answer.—No. Both the parent and the master are restricted by statute laws, and judicial decisions, to the use of such means only as are necessary and proper to secure obedience. Both parents and masters are responsible to the State for the exercise of means that are improper and unnecessary to secure this end.

Question.—Why does the law give freedom to the white race at the age of twenty-one, and withhold it from the black race during life?

Answer.—Because experience teaches that the white race can be prepared in that time to take charge of families, and perform the duties of citizens; while, on the other hand, experience demonstrates that the black race cannot be prepared during a whole life to take charge of families, or perform the duties of citizens.

Question.—But if they could be prepared in that time to use freedom for their own good, and that of the community, would it be right to accord it to them?

Answer.—It certainly would accord with Christian obligation. The only safe guide we have in a family, or State, by which to decide the amount of self-control or freedom to which men or minors are entitled under any form of government, is experience: that, and that only, will tell us how much of freedom they can use as a good to themselves, in subordination to the general good of the family, or State. When freedom is not a good to both, it is a duty to withhold it.

Question.—If self-control constitutes freedom, and control by another constitutes what is properly called slavery, then is not every person to the extent of that control a slave, whether he be called free or bond?

Answer.—Certainly he is a slave, whether so called, or not. The name does not always indicate truly the actual condition of persons in a particular relation of life.

Question.—Is the citizen who owes allegiance to the State for life, as properly a slave to the State for life, as the African, who owes service or labor to his master for life?

Answer.—Certainly, he is as much a slave to the State, though he be called a freeman. The State subjects men while within her jurisdiction to her control, and claims a right to their service in whatever form she may in her sovereignty be pleased to call for it; so the master subjects his slave to his control, and claims a right to his service in whatever form he may call for it.

Question.—But is not this service or labor to the State, and this subjection to her authority, all voluntary on the part of the white race?

Answer.—It is not more voluntary with the white minor, and the female half of the white race, than with the black slave. Both may quietly submit to it, while neither may like it. The white minor and the black slave are both born equally subject to absolute control without their consent. Both are born in a state of domestic bondage, one for life to his master, the other for twenty-one years to his father. When this age is reached, he who has been in domestic bondage up to this time, silently acquiesces in subjection to the State, which now binds him for the balance of his life to service and subjection, as the African is bound to his master for the balance of his life. The State, who is the master of the citizen, and the man, who is the master of the slave, is rightfully clothed with authority the world over to maintain dominion over both. This authority, or power to govern them, is from God. It was given to Adam before the first child was born. God said to Eve that Adam should rule over her. This included the family and the State. From my knowledge of both races in the United States, I am of opinion that the per cent. of Africans who are satisfied with their domestic bondage, is much greater than the per cent. of the white race who are satisfied with their political bondage.

Question.—How is this to be accounted for?

Answer.—Because domestic bondmen are parts of families for whose comfort ample provision is made. They are supplied with good homes, with all the necessary wants of themselves and their families for life, in sickness and in health, in infancy and in old age,—with an entire exemption from anxious care; while political bondage subjects the citizen to pecuniary burdens and an oppressive competition, which leaves him too often without a home and a comfortable supply for his necessary wants. In addition to this, political bondage subjects the citizen to all the perils attendant upon war, and a due execution of the law, from all of which the African slave, in domestic bondage, is entirely exempted.

Question.—But if "all men are born free and equal," does it not follow that children must be released from parental authority and service, apprentices from service and subjection to masters, and citizens from subjection to States, as soon as slaves from subjection and service to their masters?

Answer.—Yes, all this follows as a necessary consequence if all men are born free and equal.

Question.—Well, is it not true that all men are born free and equal?

Answer.—No. Every man who ever raised, or saw an infant man raised to manhood, knows that it is not true.

Question.—What is freedom?

Answer.—It is defined to be "independence," "liberty," "exemption from control." Man, when born, is the most dependent creature on earth. He must be deprived of all liberty, to save his life.

Question.—Can he be deprived of all liberty, and still be free?

Answer.—He must be controlled in every thing.

Question.—Is he still exempt from control?

Answer.—There has never been an assertion made and believed, which all might know with so much certainty to be untrue. Man, when born, is helplessly dependent; free to do nothing without permission, and entirely under parental control, until he is given up to the control of the State, which holds him under control until death. If this constitutes freedom, then all men are born free, but not otherwise.

The second thing affirmed in this Declaration of Independence, and, which with the above error, has been adopted by a portion of our countrymen as a part of their Bible, is, that "all men are born equal." I will only reply in language which all men know to be true, that they are not born intellectually equal; that they are not born morally equal; that they are not born politically equal; that they are not born equal in social position, or advantages; nor are they in any other sense equal, as integral parts of earthly governments, of which I can conceive, from their birth until their death. And yet a belief in these abstractions, these palpable falsehoods, is at the bottom of a crusade against organized society and constitutional liberty in the United States, which aims at the destruction of all the safeguards of life and property, and a universal overthrow of law and order, save that of the "higher law" of every murderer's conscience. We have lately had a specimen of the conscience which this "higher law" produces. It was exhibited in the person of John Brown and a few others.

This specimen is much admired by all of the same faith and order—so much so, that he is regarded by them as the second Saviour of the world,—who is destined to be as much honored for substituting his own conscience for the Bible, as Jesus Christ has been for giving eternal life to them that love him; and who prove that love, as the Bible directs, by yielding a willing obedience to law and order in all the relations of life. And because of this assumed freedom and equality, with certain assumed unalienable rights, the conclusion is drawn, according to this new political Bible, that all good government must originate in the consent of the governed. But seeing—as we all must see—that none are born either free or equal; and that subjection to government from birth is a universal necessity; it is not true that government originates in the consent of the governed. The African slave is as free to choose his government as the white minor, until the white minor reaches twenty-one years of age. At that age he *acquires* a right, in most of our States, to make, or aid in making improvements in the laws; but he can never acquire a right to abolish government, for that is God's ordinance, and cannot be rightfully abolished.

Two questions are appropriate at this point:—What is government? And what is its origin?

Answer.—Government is control; it is the opposite of freedom, or a right to do as we please. It is power to compel obedience to the will of a superior. Where did it originate? It originated in the will of God; and was ordained as soon as sin entered into the world, by an express delegation of power to Adam to rule his family. Family government is the true model of all government. There never has been, or can be a family where it does not co-exist. If societies or nations were all dissolved, this government would still exist. Its powers, objects, and administration would remain the same.

Family government is a necessity in nature. Every new family instinctively assumes it because it is God's ordinance. It is the best model of a State. Here the principles and objects of government are first learned. Without this school the idea of government could not be known.

Adam's family were parts of himself; and so of all families. This is the Divine guarantee for a right use of family authority. The impulses of nature constitute the guarantee that the divinely constituted head will rule the family in righteousness, and not abuse his authority in chastizing for disobedience.

Family government cannot be dispensed with; without it, the world would be depopulated. It is the nursery and school-room in which the materials for large families or States, must of necessity be prepared. A well-governed family is the best model for a State which exists among men. It is in the family that every human being learns the nature, the necessity, and the objects of government, and the necessity for such modifications as *experience* suggests. Here we learn that government must begin in absolute despotism, instead of absolute freedom. Here we learn that all men are born slaves to parents, that parents have a right to their service; and a right to control them until they are qualified to raise families, and use political freedom. All self-control, which is freedom, is cruelty to the infant man, and utterly inconsistent with doing to others "as we would they should do unto us." It is here we learn to what extent authority may be relaxed in subordination to the general good, that what would be a good to one would be an evil to another; that the object of government is to prevent the evil, to promote the good, and to educate the body and mind. It is here we learn that the government suited to one individual, or family, would be very unsuitable to another. That the amount of self-control to which some members entitle themselves in a family, can never be safely granted to others. It is in the family we learn to love each other, to sympathize with each other, to do justice, to speak truth, what virtue is, what vice is, what personal and property rights are, what law is, what authority is, and how, and why it should be used in enforcing law. It is here we learn that age ought to control infancy, that wisdom ought to control ignorance, and that liberty of action and opinion should be accorded by a standard that experience only can furnish. It is in the family that we learn that there is a God, our responsibility to Him, and the principles contained in his word for the moral and social control of the world. It is here we learn the qualifications which fit us to raise families, and meet the responsibilities of political freedom. And here we learn that wisdom, experience, and the highest degree of interest in the well-being of those to be governed, are necessary qualifications in those who govern. This government has been sanctioned by the States of the Federal Union for every white family and their slaves.

If we war against domestic, or family government, because it claims service or labor of the African slave for life, and subjects him to the control of a master, must we not, for the same reason, wage war against it for exacting service or labor from our children, and subjecting them to our control until they are twenty-one years old? And must we not wage war against all governments which sanction the same principle, and do the same thing, as every government has done since the world began? And when this war is successfully ended against all control, except our own wills, or the new conscience of the "higher law" Bible, will there be any government left on earth to control, or prevent any being from doing all that a depraved nature may prompt him to do?

But it is said that slavery is unjust; inasmuch as it takes from the slave his labor, and the control of himself, both of which it is said belong to him. Let use examine this objection.

Question.—What is justice?

Answer.—Locke says, "it is that virtue by which we give to every man that which is his due." Shakspeare says "it is retribution;" which Bacon defines to be, "return accommodated to the action." Both definitions claim for the slave—whether the white minor, or the black African—an equivalent for the service they render, and the submission to which they are subjected.

It is perfect folly to ignore the analogy between the slavery of our children and that of the African, and claim for our children a legal exemption from a condition of slavery as complete and perfect as that of the African slave.

The service or labor of our child is legally our money; we can coerce this labor at home—we can hire out this labor to another—or we can sell it at any price it will command in the market; and by such sale we pass to the purchaser our authority to control our child, by all necessary and proper means for that end, until he is twenty-one years old. This, and no more, is true of the African slave, except as to the length of time he serves. The service or labor of our slave, is legally our money for life. The service or labor of our child, is legally our money for twenty-one years. We can hire this service or labor of our slave to another, just as we can that of our child; or we can sell it for life, just as we can that of our child for twenty-one years; and with this service or labor we pass to the purchaser our authority to control our slave, just as we do our child—and by means only for that end which are necessary and proper.

Now for this service or labor and for this subjection and control what does the child receive on the one hand, and what does the African slave receive on the other, that makes this slavery just? Unless they both receive in return "what is due"—or, "what is accommodated to the action," then this slavery of our children and of Africans is unjust.

What does our child receive as a compensation for his labor and subjection to our control for twenty-one years? He receives a sleepless and untiring watch-care from his birth, night and day, in sickness and in health, in prosperity and adversity, until he is twenty-one years old. He receives also an exemption from all care;—food to eat, and raiment to put on; a home to shield him and a hand to defend him, a teacher to instruct and a friend to restrain him; until his mental and physical nature is sufficiently developed, and his character and habits sufficiently formed, to take the responsibilities of life on himself; or in other words, to provide for and govern a family, and meet the demands of political freedom. For all of this, which commences with his first breath, and intermits not for a moment; that has for its object the formation of character, and the acquisition of habits which will make him a blessing to himself and the world; the parent receives about eight years' service, and the most of that worth but little, from the fact that skill and strength have first to be acquired for every species of labor which has any value to the parent for the present, or to the child hereafter.

Now to say that this child does not receive in all this, more than justice demands, as a reward for his service or labor, and for his filial obedience, is what no man can say who desires to honor his own understanding. If these views be correct as regards our children, then the slavery to which they are subjected for twenty-one years is not unjust; and if slavery for twenty-one years can be just, upon the ground that the slave receives what is his due,—and that in a form "accommodated to the action," or service rendered,—then it follows that slavery for a longer time, or for the whole of life, may, for the same reason, be just also.

The Almighty has subjected all of Adam's posterity to a state of slavery as they are born into the world. Instead of giving them at their birth full-grown maturity and freedom, which was as easy for infinite wisdom and Almighty power, He ordained helplessness at their birth,—delegated power to Adam to rule over them—and then by a necessity growing out of this helplessness, compelled him to take charge of them, until their physical and intellectual natures could be educated to take charge of themselves.

The Divine constitution of things on which social happiness and prosperity are made to depend, is adapted to this condition of helpless dependence at our birth, and the want of equality in every individual of the species. In this constitution of things there is a harmonious blending of unequals. Instead of created *equality*, which does not exist among men—and which can be found nowhere, we find created *inequality* everywhere; and this *inequality* among men, is made of God to be the *cohesive element* which binds all together in the social body; so that the head cannot say to the feet, I have no need of thee; so that the least honorable make up but one social body without any schism—all the members equally needful, and harmoniously blending in the production of results which can never be reached by the control of any principle, which refuses subordination, subjection, and dependence among the various members.

In the family, which is the oldest and most important social organization, inequality, in every respect, is found to exist among all the members. Some have endowments to advance the general welfare; some are so dwarfed as to be incapable of a higher function than that of executing what another contrives; some have powers fitting them for control—others have qualities fitting them for humble submission and grateful dependence. In this most ancient organization, experience unfolds the principles for constructing a social body out of parts unequal, by which each member shall be rendered useful, made a contributor to the general welfare, and a partaker in the general result to the full amount of his due.

It is in the family that individuals learn *dependence upon each other*—how they can help each other, and how they can injure each other. It is here that our moral nature is trained to "weep with them that weep," and to "rejoice with them that do rejoice." Here we learn to love each other, and to be grateful. Here the kind offices have been practised which bind the heart of the grown man to the decrepitude of him who has watched his infancy, controlled his boyhood, and elevated him to manhood. It is on this theatre that the thrilling events and cheering reminiscences have been acted, which bind brother to brother, and sister to sister, children to parents, and man to man. It is here we learn the *measure of incapacity* which *disqualifies for the* higher responsibilities, and political and constitutional freedom; and it is pre-eminently true, that this school alone can teach us the measure of freedom with which the African slave can be invested, consistently with his own good and that of the community. The knowledge thus gained testifies that the domestic slavery of the United States accords to him all the freedom that is justly due to him, or that could be accorded on Christian principles—and that he should be held in that condition until his pupilage has developed the requisite qualifications for using more enlarged freedom.

The white child is held to service and control until he is supposed to be qualified to use political and constitutional freedom. This freedom, when it is accorded to him at the age of twenty-one, is accorded on the supposition that he is qualified to use it. If, upon trial, however, this supposition proves to be a mistake in the case of an individual, the State reserves to herself the right to withdraw his constitutional and political freedom, and to subject him to such a system of slavery or servitude, as in her judgment is best adapted to promote his own good, and that of the State; and to continue that state of slavery or servitude for any length of time which the State thinks will best subserve this end. This slavery to the State may consist in rendering service or labor in the penitentiary, in the work-house, or to a domestic master for a price to the State which he shall pay for this service, which belongs of right to the State. All this shows that the reason for which persons should be subjected to slavery in any form, for limited or unlimited periods, is because they are unfit to use freedom as a good to themselves, in subserviency to the good of the community.

We have shown why slavery is just to minors; that they received as much, or more, than they were justly entitled to; and in a form best accommodated to the service and subjection rendered, as an equivalent for it. It remains to be shown that domestic slavery for life is just and proper for the African race—because they are not qualified to use political freedom, and because they receive the full due for this service and labor, and that in a form accommodated to the service they pay for it.

The African race is constitutionally inferior to the white race. Experience proves this in all the conditions and countries they have ever occupied. The African has left no memorial which proves his capacity to improve, unaided by a superior race, or to progress when improvement has been given him. There is a great physical, moral, and intellectual difference between the two races. The tendency upon each race of the same set of circumstances, does not diminish, but increases this difference through life. The age of twenty-one, which gives bodily maturity to both races, develops moral and intellectual manhood in the white race, while the African remains, at the end of that time, a mere child in intellectual and moral development, perfectly incapable of performing the great functions of social life. By nature he is contented everywhere in destitution, until want pinches him. In freedom, he cannot be educated to provide for his present wants—much less to lay by him in store for the future. It is the present only that excites him to action. No wages will secure habitual and continued labor from him, while he is free to consult his own will. He can imitate, but cannot originate any thing. He can execute, but cannot contrive. By nature he is affectionate to his master, and if he has a good one, will separate from wife and children sooner than from him; so will a wife from her husband and children. He intuitively looks up to the superior race for control and protection. In slavery he yields hearty submission to authority, and is as proud of a rich master, as if his master's wealth were all his own. He instinctively turns from the poor white man, unless he shows by his manners that he has been well raised. The slave looks with disgust upon the free negro, because of his poverty and rags, and because he lacks those qualities which entitle freedom to respect. As a general rule, he refuses marriage with a free negro, because of his merited degradation in society. The slaves have no aspirations for political freedom, or freedom of any kind, except freedom to do nothing.

A universal tendency is seen in those slaves who have been advanced in civilization, to retrograde under the influence of freedom when it is bestowed on them; and this tendency is seldom arrested until it reaches the lowest level. It would be difficult to find an exception to this general rule, and more so, to find an instance of progressive improvement after freedom is obtained. One trait in their character in the United States corresponds in a remarkable degree with their native character in Africa; that is, an affectionate loyalty to their master. They will stand by him here, and in Africa, to the death against foreign enemies. In the war of the Revolution, and in that of 1812, they stood by their masters' defenceless wives and children, as a wall of fire for their protection and defence against the British and Tories. The same fidelity was shown by them in the late attempt to alienate them at Harper's Ferry. They form an exception in this respect to all other races of men. Their loyalty may be measured by their amount of intelligence. Their intelligence has regularly progressed since they first landed on this continent. As their intelligence increases, so does their devotion to the white race, and to the relation they sustain to that race. Hence, at the present time, a large per cent. of African intelligence repudiates freedom, and for reasons so sensible, and so unanswerable, as to make misguided philanthropy blush for its want of sound, practical common sense. Their answer to the sophistry of this spurious benevolence is always at hand, and will continue to be so, as long as free negroes are to be found in their present condition everywhere on the globe. They have acquired a pretty correct knowledge of what they cannot see at a distance, and that confirms them in the opinion they have formed from what they do see around them—and that opinion is, that as a race, the protection, control, and social advantages of the white race are a positive necessity to them, and that they are worth more to them as a race, than their service or labor can be to the white race, after abstracting for themselves a full supply for every want during the vicissitudes of an entire life. And with the permission and encouragement of their masters, they would exterminate the agents who come among us to alienate them from their allegiance.

My purpose, thus far, has been to show that African slavery in the United States is a social and political necessity, and to show that it is just to the African, as it accords to him, in a form best adapted to his nature, more than an equivalent for his service, or labor; and that it is in accordance with the obligation to "do good to all men," and to "do to others as we would they should do unto us."

If the question of enslaving free Africans on the continent of Africa were an open one, it would aid us, before deciding it, to suppose a case. A free African infant on that continent, endowed with the intelligence of manhood, is approached by one of the white race, who proposes hereditary bondage to him and his posterity, and as an equivalent to him for the loss of his liberty, offers him the following compensation: If you will allow me to control you and your posterity, I will give you in return what will be worth more to you and to them, than your freedom and the avails of your labor. I will guarantee to you and to them, from the cradle until death, the benefit of all the endowments of the white race, in the following particulars: First, an unceasing watch-care shall be given to your persons; second, the best medical skill shall be furnished you when sick; third, the best surroundings of sympathy and kindness shall be secured to you when afflicted; fourth, good homes and houses secured to you for life; fifth, good and suitable clothing shall be furnished you to put on; sixth, you shall have a bountiful supply of food at all times to eat; seventh, you shall be protected from insult and injury; eighth, you shall be relieved from all anxious care; ninth, you shall be shielded from the perils of war, and the burdens of government; tenth, you shall be furnished with gospel instruction; eleventh, you shall enjoy the benefits and blessings of the best school in the world, that of domestic association for life with a superior order of honorable and cultivated men and women. By their example, and their superior intellects, you will learn lessons of more real value to you than all the books and schoolmasters on the globe could ever teach you, while you stand in any other relation to this superior race, than that of being a part and parcel of their family, working for their benefit, and subjected to their control and government. This control and government are the same to which their children are subjected, while being trained up to maturity and manhood. If you cannot reach the same attainments they do, you can make yourself welcome as a part of their families by the discharge of your duty, and can share with them in all the advantages which can rightfully be accorded to your attainments. And all the progressive attainments you may make in this school, shall continue to be rewarded with the advantages which justice may claim for them.

This young African subsequently replies: Since your proposal, I have had a review of the world's history, covering a period of more than three thousand years. During all this time, I have seen that my race in Africa—so prolific in every thing that makes up the catalogue of human comfort, with all the advantages of a climate peculiarly adapted to the health of my race,—yet I have seen that they have remained a mass of moral degradation and stolid ignorance, sinking lower and lower in the scale of intelligence and civilization, until, upon its southern half (stretching from the Equator to the Cape of Good Hope) all knowledge of God, of immortality, of sin, of right and wrong, of heaven and hell, which originally they must have brought with them, is entirely lost; and instead of settled homes to raise their children, and an organized system to supply their wants and protect their lives, they have become, by day, homeless, roving vagabonds, picking up something as chance may favor, to support life; and brutes by night, piled up like hogs, in holes they scratch in the sand, to rest their naked bodies. While its northern half, (stretching from the Equator to the Mediterranean,) with slight exceptions, is one great graveyard, enclosing unnumbered millions of the dead of my race, who have been sacrificed by war and famine for the privilege of making slaves of their brothers and sisters, and their own children, without the slightest advance in civilization.

I have learned, also, from the Christian's Bible, that the Being who made this world, once destroyed by a flood of water all its inhabitants for their wickedness, except one man named Noah, and his three sons, Shem, Ham, and Japheth, and their wives. Ham, my father, was a compound of beastly wickedness. I learned from this Book that these three sons were types of nations, that were to spring from them to repeople the earth. The descendants of Shem were to be distinguished for the blessed God they worshipped, whose character and perfections it was their mission to make known to all others; and that the descendants of Ham, my father, were made their servants. The descendants of Japheth were distinguished for a progressive intelligence, and a commanding influence upon the destinies of the world. These qualities were to give them dominion in the tents of Shem, and the descendants of Ham were made their servants. And this future elevation of Japheth to the dominion of the world, was to harmonize with supreme reverence for that God whom they had been brought to know by dwelling in the tents of Shem, whose God was the eternal I AM, and not dumb idols.

The descendants of Ham, the beastly and degraded son of Noah, were subjected to a degraded servitude to Shem and Japheth.

After this I learned that slavery was spread over the whole globe, embracing the descendants of Shem, Ham, and Japheth. I learned, also, that subsequently freedom was extended in many nations to the descendants of Shem and Japheth, and last of all, to some of the descendants of Ham, my father. I was astonished at the result. The emancipated descendants of Shem and Japheth invariably made progress, and reached higher attainments in freedom. My race invariably retrograded from the position they had reached under the enlightened control of Shem or Japheth. The invariable tendency of freedom was to sink them to the level of their original degradation.

Now, I will not make a decision for this young African on the continent of Africa; but I will say, that all enlightened manhood, which thinks it unjust and sinful to subject such helpless and hopeless moral and social degradation to intelligent and human control, and invest it with the social and religious advantages of the slavery of this Union—dishonors the human understanding, the best instincts of our nature, and is utterly unfit to take charge of a nation's welfare.

The picture drawn expresses sober historical truth with respect to Ham's sons when invested with freedom on the one hand, and American bondage on the other. Exceptions may be found to the general rule of good treatment to the slave in the United States; so they may in all the relations existing among men. The relation of husband and wife should secure kindness to the wife; yet the per cent. of husbands, where slavery does not exist, who abuse their authority and neglect their duty to their wives, I set down, from all the information I can get, as greater than the per cent. of masters at the South who abuse their authority and neglect their duty to their slaves. The per cent. of fathers, within the range of exclusive freedom, who abuse their authority over their children, or who use it without regard to the object for which it was given of God, I set down, from all the data I can command, as greater than the per cent. of Southern masters, who do the same thing to their slaves. The per cent. of free white families at the North, for whose comfort there is not a regular and proper provision made by their domestic heads, is greater than the number of slave families whose Southern masters have failed to make such a provision for them. The per cent. of white families, for whose condition in infancy, sickness, and old age, there is not suitable medical aid and sympathetic attention provided by their domestic heads, is perhaps many thousand times greater at the North, than the per cent. of slave families who are unprovided by their Southern masters with these indispensable blessings. Among four millions of slaves at the South there is not one pauper, although one-fourth of their lives they are helpless, either from the weakness of infancy, or the infirmities of old age. At the North, every seventh family is without a home, and in the cities, one-fifth of the persons must receive help or perish; while four millions of slaves at the South have good homes, and three plentiful meals of good food provided for them, by their masters, every day—with comfortable clothing, and an unlimited supply of fuel for fires, in winter. Such a provision as this has never been secured to any equal number of free laborers on the globe. It is perfectly horrifying to a Southern slave-owner to read the statistics of poverty, vice, and suffering, where money is the master of labor. The skill and industry of the white race, in general, justly entitle them to a comfortable provision for life; but, within the boundaries of exclusive freedom, cupidity and the power of money withhold it as soon as the supply of free labor exceeds the demands of capital. That state of things often happens with slave labor and capital at the South; but, then, the slave's wages are not diminished: neither is he dismissed to perish of want, or to sell himself to work wickedness.

Slavery, or control by the will of another, in some form, and to the extent which varying circumstances make proper, is now, and has been in all ages, an indispensable necessity. Too large a measure or too great an abridgment of liberty is equally fatal to the welfare of a people and to the happiness of individuals. The elementary principle which should control a wise settlement of the proper amount of freedom to classes or individuals, under any form of government, whether family, State, or Federal, is best learned in rearing and governing a family. Here experience becomes the basis of theory; and not theory the basis of practice. Here we learn that of the white race, in the highest forms of civilization, about seven-eighths of the number to be governed are subjected, without their consent in any form, to the control and government of about one-eighth of the individuals who make up the families or States. One half, being females, are so subjected for life; and three-fourths of the other half, being minors, are so subjected for a term of years. The remaining fourth are all that can be said, in any sense of the word, to be governed by their own wills—and, when formed into States, they are slaves, or what is the same, are subjected to the control of their own State law, and are as liable to its burdens and penalties as any other class of persons. The reason and the propriety of enslaving or controlling this large majority by this small minority are so obvious, that no government within the pale of Christian civilization has ever been constructed without being controlled by the reason which makes it proper. What is that reason? *It is*, that the portion thus excluded from the governing power are not qualified to exercise this power, with safety to themselves or others. In that *disqualification, the propriety is found* of withholding this power from them; and of subjecting them to the control of those who are qualified to govern. In this state of facts—disclosed by the experience of all ages —originate all the varying forms of involuntary servitude found among men. The principles of righteousness lend their full sanction to the control which subordinates individual freedom to the general good, and accords to individuals only the amount they can use as a good. By this standard of measuring the right and the wrong of slavery, of freedom, and of government, African slavery in the United States ought to be tested. Whenever it is so tested, it will be found to be right for the white race—just and humane for the black race—expedient and proper for both races—and in accordance with the highest responsibilities of Christian freemen.

So far as the capacity of the African has yet been developed, we have no reason to believe they can retain the blessings of civilization and the gospel which we have given them, when our control and protection are withdrawn. The evidence which sustains this conclusion, stares the civilized world in the face, like the sun in the heavens.

On this continent, at an early stage of our history, well meant efforts were permitted in the providence of God, the object of which was to bless Ham's race by releasing them from our control, and giving them freedom. These efforts have gone on among well-meaning men for more than two centuries. For the whole of this time, facts have been accumulating, which prove *their freedom to be a curse*, both to them and the white race. Still, additional aids, suggested by benevolence, have been resorted to by good men in the slave States, to make the experiment successful, until the demonstration seems complete, that freedom to them is a curse on this continent, and everywhere else on the globe. These untiring efforts on the part of benevolent individuals, have been in silent progress in the slave States, and are but little known by those at a distance. Their voice is the voice of God. *He thus proclaims to us, that in these efforts we are warring against His fixed plan.* Misguided philanthropy, however, still found excuses for the failure. That failure, it was thought, would not have taken place upon a fair field for the experiment. To meet this bewitching blindness of benevolent slaveholders at the South, God in His providence has tolerated the selection of three different theatres, more favorably situated, upon which to make the experiment on a large scale. Two of them he surrounded with the overflowings of sympathy, aid, and counsel, by three of the most powerful nations of the earth.

In Jamaica, one hundred millions of dollars were paid to the owners of Ham's descendants in that island by the English government, to release from bondage a set of well-fed laborers, who were supplying their own wants, rendering a remunerating income to their owners, and a needful supply of tropical productions for the wants of the mother country. Here the experiment was thoughtfully made, and surrounded by a wise forecast, that seemed to bid defiance to failure. The land was owned by the white race; their farms were all in good order; on these farms there was a supply of good houses; in these houses the slaves had lived and reared their families; these farms were supplied with the tools and machinery necessary for their successful cultivation, and to the use of these tools and this machinery the slaves had been accustomed since childhood. These farms, the houses on them, the tools and machinery, with the supervision of the owner, were the capital which England said, and believed, was to be rendered more valuable by free than by slave labor. On every farm the needed supply of labor was to be found. A moral guarantee was given to the laborer, that capital should not oppress him; because the demand of capital for labor should always be kept greater in that island than the supply. Of course, capital would be compelled to give the highest price for labor which a small return of profit would allow.

What has been the result of this well-arranged experiment, to give

An intelligent correspondent of the New York *Times*, who visited the West Indies a year ago, gave this explicit and unanswerable testimony to the beneficial effects of emancipation:

"I wish to give point-blank denial to a very general impression that the Jamaica negro will not work at all. I wish to exhibit the people of Jamaica as peaceable, law-abiding peasantry. I wish to bear witness to their courtesy. When I had occasion to ask for cocoanuts or oranges on the wayside, the settlers generally refused payment for the fruit. The district through which I have been travelling is composed entirely of pasture land. All the settlers (emancipated slaves) own a house and stock of some kind. Their cottages are very neat and tidy, and are shrouded with cocoas and plantains. In the better class of cottages, I have invariably found books—always the Bible, and not unfrequently the ponderous works of William Wilberforce.

"Quite close to one group of cottages stood a neat little Baptist chapel, built by the laborers, at their own expense. These people, who live comfortably and independently, own houses and stock, pay taxes and poll votes, and pay their money to build churches, and are the same people whom we have heard represented as idle, worthless fellows, obstinately opposed to work, and ready to live on an orange or a banana rather than earn their daily bread.

"The people are no longer servile, though they retain, from habit, the servile epithet of Massa, when addressing the whites. There is no discarding the fact, that since their freedom, no people in the world have been more peaceful than the creoles of Jamaica. With their freedom, they seem to have forgotten all ancient grievances, and never even to have thought of retaliation. The contrast, in this respect, between the reign of *freedom* and the reign of *slavery*, carries its own lesson and its own warning. Since emancipation, they have passed in a body, to a higher civil and social state. Any unprejudiced resident in Jamaica will indorse the statement here made, that the peasantry are as peaceful and industrious a people as may be found in the same latitude throughout the world. The present generation of Jamaica creoles is no more to be compared to their slave ancestors, than the intelligent English laborer of the nineteenth century can be compared with the serfs of Athelstane or of Atheling."

freedom to this race of people? Homes were ready for every one of them—homes too in which they were raised; the highest price for labor awaited every one of them who would work; a powerful and sympathetic government threw her shield around them; the avails of their labor were secured to them, with assurance doubly sure that merit should have every thing accorded to it which justice could command. I ask again, what has been the result of this well-arranged and costly experiment, to give freedom to Ham's descendants? The result is, according to reports made to the English Parliament, (by abolition members sent in different years from their own body, to make a strict personal examination,) that the export of sugar in a short time had fallen off from upwards of six hundred millions to two thousand pounds, and very soon after to nothing; and that every other product of labor had shared the same fate. That the farms had grown over in bushes; that the ditches were filled up; that the roads were impassable; that the machinery was rusting and rotting unused; that the houses were surrounded with brushwood and trees which nearly concealed them; that thousands of negroes were hovering around the towns on the coast in destitution and starvation, whose existence was a mystery, as none could account for it; that others had retreated from civilization and the reach of law to the mountains, where they were living in savage and beastly degradation on roots and herbs, and that no price would secure labor. That the value of real estate was reduced, according to an assessment, twelve millions in a very short time; in short, that the island and the negroes were ruined, unless efficient control in some form was re-assumed by their well-meaning but misguided benefactors.

The second experiment, to which allusion has been made, is the one in Africa. The best materials to be found among the free negroes of the United States were selected for this experiment.

Long and anxiously in our country had the highest order of minds, the purest philanthropy, the most disinterested patriotism, and the most self-sacrificing benevolence, sought to do good to this race of people, and to originate and put in operation a practical plan for elevating them to the blessings of a higher civilization, and a more enlarged freedom, or self-control. For accomplishing their desires, these great men, so distinguished in the world's history for disinterested goodness, met in the city of Washington in 1816; and, after mature deliberation, adopted a plan for carrying out their wishes by the agency of an organization which they called "The American Colonization Society." Their purpose was, to aid free persons of color to settle a colony or colonies in Africa. In pursuance of this plan, they raised by voluntary contribution a sufficient fund, employed suitable agents to explore the coast, and finally purchased of the natives on that continent a territory large enough for the settlement of every negro, free and bond, in the United States.

To this well selected home—rich in soil, salubrious in climate, and highly adapted to commerce—they commenced transporting such of Ham's descendants in the United States as were most advanced in civilization, public spirit, and intelligence.

So great was the desire of Southern philanthropists to succeed in this experiment, that through their influence indirect aid was obtained from the Federal Government, to sustain the infant colony against the hostile natives. Places of defence were built by the aid of our sailors, and the presence of our war ships afforded security against aggression.

The passage of the emigrants to their new home, six months' provision when they arrived there, lands surveyed and ready for settlement, hospitals for the sick, and medical aid for their assistance, were all thoughtfully arranged and secured to them by these noble-hearted men. But the above catalogue of bounty falls far short of the whole-souled benevolence and forethought which characterized their efforts. The society and its influence secured for the colonists all kinds of tools to cultivate their fields, carts and wagons for the use of their farms, steam mills to saw their lumber, to grind their grain, and to manufacture their cane into sugar and molasses, draft animals to plough their land, arms to defend their persons by land, and ships for their commerce by sea.

They provided for them a government free of charge, and secured for them, either directly or indirectly, school-houses and teachers for their children, churches in which to worship God, Bibles and preachers to teach them the way to heaven, books filled with instruction on all suitable subjects, printing-presses to diffuse knowledge, clothing for their bodies, and affectionate and enlightened counsel for their minds. Thousands of hearts, in all parts of our country, ascended to God for their success, and followed them to their new homes, in every form of benevolence. Our Government has indirectly secured them against hostility and violence, at an expense, if fairly estimated, that would reach many millions of dollars. Every motive was quickened into activity which could be awakened in their hearts, for the regeneration of Africa, and their own progress in Christian civilization.

Could a better theatre have been selected—could better materials have been secured to occupy it—could wiser and better counsellors have been selected on the globe, to guide their infant movements in the mission of self-improvement and African redemption?

The noblest branch of Japheth's descendants, who had been so long accustomed to progress on this continent, were slow to doubt the success of this experiment, and could not patiently and wisely weigh the evidence time began to furnish, that its success was doubtful. Whether by design or not, discouraging facts were withheld from the public, and flattering pictures of success were given to the world.

Our country was made familiar by the press with comparisons between this and other colonizing experiments, with a large balance in favor of Liberia. Yet in 1843, more than twenty years after the settlement of the colony, their statistics showed that the average quantity of land cultivated in this agricultural colony (including town lots) was about one-third of an acre per head; and that not a single draft animal, plough, wagon, or cart, was used at that time for any purpose; that no farming tool was used except a bill-hook and hoe. That the machinery sent them to saw their lumber, grind their grain, and manufacture their cane into sugar and molasses, and the tools sent them to cultivate their lands, were then rusting and rotting unused. The colonists have at all times affirmed that the soil was exceedingly productive, yet their custom-house, at that time, reported not a single article exported from Liberia, which was produced by the labor of the colonists. The articles for which their soil was peculiarly adapted, such as tobacco, breadstuffs, cotton, coffee, sugar, molasses, potatoes, &c., were imported from abroad, and so was their meat. All these articles commanded high prices in their own market, prices which ought to have induced their cultivation by any human being willing to labor.

After they had been adding to the outfit which they carried with them, the avails of their own labor, and all that had been given them by their benefactors for more than twenty years, the assessed value of their agricultural wealth was five dollars and a few cents per head. During the whole of this time their government had cost them nothing, and our navy had given them peace and security.

Statements however were in conflict, and its friends from time to time sought for information that certainly could be relied on. The last accredited agent was Mr. Cowen from the Kentucky Colonization Society, who in 1858, after a sojourn of seven weeks, made a report. This report, with respect to agriculture, presents about the same state of facts as those of 1843. The colonists have always affirmed that the climate was healthy, yet with a rich soil to give them food, and a healthy climate to prolong their lives, and forty years to multiply their race, they are now about one-fifth less in number than the original emigrants.

The general view I have taken of Jamaica and Liberia is derived from sources that are entitled to the highest credit; but my information has been obtained from different sources and at different times, and was not carefully preserved, supposing it could be obtained again at pleasure from historical records, and in chronological order; but in this I was mistaken. There is nothing, however, in point of *fact*, from any quarter, tending to a different conclusion from that at which I have arrived; that is, that this race of people have never as yet proved themselves capable, under any circumstances, of retaining in freedom what slavery gives them; or of making progressive improvement, unless they are subject more or less to the control of the white race. For more than three years, I have been trying to get statistical and historical facts concerning these experiments on foreign fields. But the library of Congress, the proprietors of book-stores, and some of the best informed of our public men, could give me no aid. This is a suggestive fact. "He that doeth truth, cometh to the light," says Christ. Here are experiments that have been in progress for more than forty years, one of them by the most enlightened government in the world, the other by many of the most enlightened individuals in the United States, that are almost covered up in darkness. Why is this?

One of the ordinances of God is, that man shall eat bread in the sweat of his face; that is, that he shall by labor contribute his share to the common stock of supply for human wants. Christ has ordained that, in his kingdom, no man shall eat unless he work. We have sent Ham's descendants to Africa to raise and govern families, and to assume the higher responsibilities of organizing and governing states. From the best authenticated facts we can gain, we are obliged to believe they are not qualified to do either, because they will not perform voluntary labor. Among Ham's race in freedom, here and elsewhere, there are but a few individuals who are willing to labor continuously for the support of a family. No people can multiply and raise families, unless they have homes, and are well fed. In the Northern States, in Jamaica, and in Liberia, the deaths among the free blacks steadily exceed the births. The slaves at the South multiply faster than the white race at the North.

On the field of experiment there is another that deserves our notice. In Hayti, the slaves were emancipated by the Assembly of France in 1793. In the same year they slaughtered the white race, and appropriated to themselves the invested wealth of the island. This island had been in a most prosperous condition before that event. Its exported productions had been immense. From that time its productions declined, and from the address of their President last year, they have reached the lowest level of laziness and poverty, are in a very degraded condition, as much, or more so than the original inhabitants when the island was discovered by Columbus in 1492.

I have said the evidence which proves the unfitness of the African for freedom, stares us in the face as the sun in the heavens—that it amounts to a demonstration. That evidence has been passed in review before my reader. It consists first, in the experiment at the South, of giving freedom to the most promising of the race. We of the South know that it has proved a curse to them. It has involved them in a little more than ten times the amount of crime, and a measure of poverty destructive of all comfort. An unwillingness to labor is almost universal among them.

The North emancipated that portion of the race they held in bondage. From the same unwillingness to labor they are too poor to raise families, are diminishing in numbers, and are degraded by an amount of crime which exceeds more than twelve times that of the white race.

In Jamaica, no wages can overcome their unwillingness to perform labor.

In Liberia, where they have been literally held up by kindness and counsel, and stimulated by the prospect of regenerating Africa, we see the same incurable disease.

In Hayti, we see them sharing all the evils which flow from self-control and an unwillingness to labor, while we see the slaves at the South, under the control of the white race, contented and well provided for, increasing in numbers, and improving in morals and intelligence.

What I have written thus far was intended to disabuse men's minds as to the origin of government, as to its "resting on the consent of the governed,"—as to being "born free and equal," as to what constitutes slavery, as to what constitutes freedom, as to the rule by which freedom or self-control is to be meted out; as to the propriety, in civilized life, of subjecting seven-eighths of the human family to the control of one-eighth; as to the justice of according freedom to the white race at a given age, and withholding it from Africans for life; as to the evidence furnished that they are an inferior race, and unfit for social and political freedom.

In my next, slavery will be tested by the Bible, as a question of morals and a divinely appointed element in the social and religious progress of the world.

CHAPTER II.

Teachings of the Bible—The world re-peopled after the flood by three distinct races—These races all descend from one man—One of these races devoted to Slavery—The other two ordained by the Almighty to be their masters—Domestic Slavery sanctioned of God in the families of the Patriarchs—A runaway Slave returned to the owner by a special messenger from Heaven—A nation of the devoted race, who were free, enslaved by the Almighty—A nation of the free race, who were domestic slaveholders, liberated by the Almighty, from national bondage to the devoted race—A Slave Code enacted by the Almighty—Slave markets designated by Him for the purchase of Slaves—The devoted race divided into nations—Seven of these nations devoted to utter destruction, the balance of them to Slavery—Divine authority, that Slavery is in harmony with the moral precept, which requires us "to love our neighbor as ourself"—The extent and character of Slavery when Christ came—All Governments at that time sanctioned Slavery—What Christ in person did, and taught his disciples to do, in reference to governments.

Having, in the preceding chapter, attempted to show that slavery is nothing more nor less than control by the will of another, and that this control is an indispensable necessity from our birth until our physical, moral, and intellectual faculties are sufficiently developed for the responsibilities of social and political life; and that this development is generally reached by the white race in about twenty-one years, and that it has never as yet been reached by the black race at any age, either on this continent or anywhere else, of which we have knowledge; and having assigned that as a true, proper, and sufficient reason for holding them under the control of the white race, both as a good to that race and themselves,—I will now proceed to examine slavery by the Bible, as a question of morals. It will be of service to those who reverence the Bible, but who do not know what it teaches, or where to look for its teachings on the subject of slavery, to sum up a portion of them on that subject, and refer to the books, chapter, and verses, where they may be found.

In Gen. ix. 25, 26, 27, you will find that soon after the flood Ham's descendants were doomed by the Almighty to a state of slavery, and that the descendants of Shem and Japheth, by the same decree, were ordained to be their masters. From Ham descended fifteen nations, that settled between the Euphrates and the Mediterranean. Seven of these nations were devoted to utter destruction, and their land given to Abraham's seed. See Deut. xx. 16, 17, and Deut. vii. 1, 2. The remaining eight nations were to be subjected by Abraham's seed to *national bondage.* See Deut. xi. 24, and xx. 10, 11. If they would not submit to national bondage, when summoned, then the males were all to be destroyed, and the females subjected to *domestic bondage.* See Deut. xx. 12 to 18. When these eight nations were subjected by Abraham's seed to *national bondage*, their authority over them was not to stop at political subjection; they were to expurgate these nations of idolatry for the true worship of Abraham's God. Deut. xii. 1, 2, 3.

Abraham is the first domestic slaveholder mentioned in the Bible, and he is constantly held up to view as the most distinguished man for piety in the patriarchal age. There is a mistake frequently made by readers of the Bible, in supposing the servants of the patriarchs, and those servants instructed by the Apostles, in the New Testament, to be hired servants, and not hereditary slaves. I ask my reader to criticize the quotations as they are brought to view, by the references which follow, that he may see for himself that this mistake has no foundation to rest upon.

When Lot was taken prisoner, Gen. xiv. 14, Abraham owned three hundred and eighteen slaves that were born in his house, old enough to bear arms. From these data, according to the usual calculation, his entire slave family, at this time, must have been upwards of fifteen hundred. Soon after this, Abraham was driven by a famine into Egypt, when the items of his principal wealth are given us, Gen. xii. 15, 16. In this catalogue his slaves form a conspicuous part as items of property. Soon after this, in a neighboring kingdom, Abraham received a large present from the reigning sovereign of the country. Among the valuable items of property which make up this gift, slaves again form a conspicuous part. See Gen. xx. 14, 15, 16. In default of children, Sarah, his wife, prevailed upon him to marry her slave maid Hagar, an Egyptian woman who was given to Sarah by Pharaoh, King of Egypt. To marry slave wives, and to have a plurality of wives, were both lawful under the law of the patriarchs. They were both made lawful four hundred years after by the law of Moses. This slave woman Hagar ran away, because of rough treatment to which she was subjected by her mistress, on account of her insolence. In the wilderness she was met by an Angel of God and ordered back, with positive directions to submit herself under her mistress's hands. See Gen. xvi. 1 to 9. The conduct of God's messenger to this down-trodden female, as our Northern brethren would call her, differs very much from their conduct at the present time. That messenger ordered the fugitive slave back to her owner—the Abolitionist refuses to deliver them up.

In Gen. xvii. a covenant is mentioned. In this covenant God gave to Abraham's seed citizenship and the land of Canaan. This covenant secured both to Abraham's male posterity through Isaac, Jacob, and twelve of Jacob's sons, excluding from citizenship and the soil Ishmael, Abraham's first born son, and Esau, Isaac's first born son, and all others forever. Not one foot of this land could be alienated. It was entailed in perpetuity on Abraham's male descendants through the above line, and with it political responsibility and power. Political power and the soil were given exclusively to them. Abraham's other children and slaves were bound by circumcision to acknowledge and worship Abraham's God. Circumcision gave religious privileges, but not national identity, or political power. Abraham was bound to impose circumcision on his children and slaves. Hence Abraham circumcised, not only Ishmael his son, but himself and all his slaves that were born in his house, or that were bought with his money of any stranger. See Gen. xvii. 23 to 26. *Question*—Could our Northern brethren hold fellowship with this old slaveholder if he were to appear among them?

The next view which the Scriptures furnish us of this distinguished slaveholder and favorite of the Almighty, is the occasion he improves of getting a wife for his son Isaac. Isaac had been designated by the Almighty as the progenitor of the Messiah—in whom all the nations of the earth were to be blessed. See Gen. xxi. 12, and xxii. 1 to 18.

Abraham intrusted this mission of getting a wife for Isaac, to the most distinguished servant he had. At an earlier period of Abraham's life, and before he had a child, he thought of making this servant, on account of his high qualities and sterling integrity, the heir of his whole estate. He now sends him on this delicate and important mission, under special instruction. He requires him to take a solemn oath to follow his directions to the very letter. He puts him in possession of all the means he was to use to insure success; jewels that were beautiful and costly for the lady, splendid presents for her family, and a catalogue of his wealth which he intended to give his son at his death. This estate the servant enumerated to the lady's family in the following words: "I am Abraham's servant, and the Lord hath blessed my master greatly, and he is become great; and he hath given him flocks and herds, and silver and gold, and men servants, and maid servants, and camels, and asses. And Sarah, my master's wife, bare a son to my master when she was old; and unto him hath he given all he hath." See Gen. xxiv. 34, 35, 36.

After this marriage of Isaac was consummated, Abraham married again, and had six sons by Keturah, besides his first-born son Ishmael by Hagar. Before his death, he sent these seven sons out of the country which God had given his posterity through Isaac. To these sons he made presents when he sent them away. But true to the message he sent by his servant to get a wife for Isaac, he gave to Isaac all that he had, and this included the land of Canaan which God had given him by promise. Gen. xxv. 5. To his other sons he gave gifts, and sent them away from Isaac, his son, (while he yet lived,) eastward, out of the promised land, unto the east country, and died in a good old age. Gen. xxv. 6, 7, 8.

Question.—Can holding men and women in bondage, giving them to our children when we die, and sharing the honor they in part give us in the sight of God and men while we live, be sinful? that is, if the word of God was written to teach us what sin is.

Soon after Abraham's death, his son Isaac made a very distinguished figure upon the stage of the world. The historical notice given of him is, that he was "a prosperous man"—"reaping an hundred fold" from the land he cultivated; that he "waxed great," "went forward," "and grew until he became very great; for he had possessions of flocks, and great store of servants." The next account we have of him is, that the citizens of the government under which he was living, *envied* him exceedingly. Why, says fanaticism, a tyrant who lives upon the sweat and blood of his fellow-man ought to be abhorred of God, and should be hated of men. Well, let us see how he stands with Abraham's God. He was then living in the kingdom of Gerar. The envy of his neighbors, who were citizens of this kingdom, made his home so disagreeable, that he removed thence, and went to Beersheba, grieved in heart that a people to whom he had done no harm should invade his home, endanger his life, and the lives of his servants—violently wrest his property from him, and render it unsafe for him to dwell among them. See Gen. xxvi. 12 to 23. But the Lord appeared to him the same night, after these painful demonstrations of unconquerable envy and hatred had caused him to separate himself from this people, and said to him, "I am the God of Abraham thy father; fear not" the malignity and lawlessness of these men, "for I am with thee, and will bless thee, and multiply thy seed." Gen. xxvi. 23, 24, 25.

The lawlessness and malignity of these people were enough to awaken the fears of this princely slaveholder. We are living under analogous circumstances. While we may not have for our comfort the direct assurance of this great slaveholder, that God will be with us, and bless us; yet, through patience and comfort of the Scriptures, we may have hope that he will.

Isaac had two sons, who were twins. He was led by a prophetic impulse to make a public transfer of the blessings of the Abrahamic covenant to one of these sons before his death. Under the influence of partial feelings and common usage, he was about to transfer these blessings to Esau. Bnt means were used by which they were unintentionally, on his part, transferred to Jacob. Isaac was duly assured by Divine impulse, after the deed was done, that it was God's will that Jacob should have this inheritance; and under prophetic inspiration he said to Jacob, "Let people serve thee, and nations bow down to thee: be lord over thy brethren, and let thy mother's sons bow down to thee: cursed be every one that curseth thee, and blessed be every one that blesseth thee." Gen. xxvii.

Jacob's subsequent history shows him to have been one of the greatest slaveholders of the age. If my views were those of an Abolitionist, I should be obliged to hate the God of Jacob, and instead of saying as God did, "Cursed be every one that *curseth thee*," my abolition views would compel me to say, "Cursed be every one that *blesseth thee*."

Soon after this transaction of blessing Jacob, Isaac, his father, called Jacob to him, gave him a charge to take a wife from a God-fearing family, and not from an idolatrous people, and then sent him away with this inspired benediction: "God Almighty bless thee, and multiply thee; and give the blessings of Abraham to thee, and to thy seed with thee; that thou mayest inherit the land wherein thou art a stranger, which God gave to Abraham." Gen. xxviii. 1 to 4.

Jacob, thus charged and thus blessed by his inspired father, went to Padan Aram, married, and lived there twenty years. The night after he left his father's house to go to Padan Aram, God appeared to him and gave him this assurance: "I am the Lord God of Abraham thy father, and the God of Isaac; the land whereon thou liest, to thee will I give, and to thy seed," (now mark the caution used here, and in every other place, to designate the heirs of the land of Canaan: they must be Abraham's male descendants through Jacob,) "and thy seed shall be as the dust of the earth; and thou shalt spread abroad to the West, and to the East, and to the North, and to the South; and in thee, and *in thy seed*, shall all the nations of the earth be blessed." Gen. xxviii. 13, 14, 15.

When Jacob, twenty years after this, was thinking of leaving Padan Aram, where he had been badly treated by his father-in-law, this is the account we have of him: "The man increased exceedingly, and had mnch cattle, and maid servants, and men servants, and camels, and asses." Gen. xxx. 43. This property in slaves which he accumulated in Padan Aram, and that which he inherited from his father soon after, made him a princely slaveholder, as his fathers had been. In all these catalogues of property owned by Abraham, Isaac, and Jacob, servants occupy the place of chattels. They were bought with their money; they were called "their money;" they were raised in their families, and were passed as an inheritance to their children in perpetuity. Hired servants are carefully distinguished from hereditary, or bond servants.

During the life of the patriarch Jacob, we are presented with a very suggestive fact in favor of enslaving a people for their own good, who are not qualified for freedom. A branch of Ham's race occupied, at that time, the fruitful valley of the Nile in Egypt. They were liable, by laziness, negligence, and a want of forethought and energy, to famine, owing to a casualty of frequent occurrence, which caused a failure in the annual crop.

To teach Ham's race a lesson, and through them the world a lesson, the Almighty allowed Jacob's son, Joseph, a descendant of Shem, to be sold into slavery in that kingdom. It was Shem's mission to preserve the knowledge, and make known the character of the true God to all nations. Shem was sent to Egypt at this time, in the person of Joseph, not only to make known the character, attributes, and perfections of the true God, but to make known the character and elements of good government among them. Joseph soon convinced Pharaoh, when brought into his presence, that essential elements were wanting in his government, that wise forethought, and an energetic control over his subjects would save them from this national calamity with which they were afflicted; that this government must be changed, and that his subjects were not qualified for self-control, or freedom. Accordingly, under impulses awakened in Pharaoh's heart, this young man was invested with authority by Pharaoh, to change the political structure of the government, by enslaving the persons, and purchasing the property, real and personal, of the whole kingdom, with the exception of the priesthood. He secured for Pharaoh an absolute right to the control, service, and labor of this people forever. A new arrangement was immediately made by Joseph for the more efficient con*rol of labor, and for a careful preservation of the surplus.

This was done by bringing a number of families together in cities, from one end of the kingdom to the other, so that a few competent overseers (men of skill, enterprise, and authoritative energy) could supervise the labor and the civil conduct of a great many persons. By this change labor was well husbanded, a bountiful supply was secured for the wants of the people, a surplus was put in store for contingencies, and a regular supply of means laid by for the support of the government.

The authority for all this is to be found in Gen. xli. to xlvii., inclusive.

Subjecting this people to slavery, was God's work. He, by a special providence of seven years' continuance, brought them into a condition that unavoidably subjected them to hereditary slavery, or to death by famine, if they refused submission to it. Now let me ask all well-meaning, honest-minded men, this question. If slavery be a sin, as the Abolitionists say it is, then why did the Almighty take advantage of the condition into which he brought this people, to deprive them of liberty, and subject them to slavery? I would answer this question by saying, God designed it for their good, and to teach them, and all others through them, that slavery was a greater good to any people than freedom, without proper qualifications to use freedom. All of this is written in the Bible for our learning—that we when called upon, in the providence of God, to arrange the best form of government for men who prove themselves incapable of self-government, (as the Africans do among us, and everywhere else with but few individual exceptions,) that we do not suffer ourselves to be led away by the infidelity which sanctions universal freedom and equality—a freedom and an equality, of which the Bible knows nothing; nor by a false humanity which takes away a good from a people, and puts an evil in the place of it—as this infidelity in the United States seeks to do, by taking from the African the protection and control of the white race, and leaving him to perish by giving him freedom to do nothing—which is the only freedom he desires.

The difference between freedom and slavery to this race of people, when the comparison is made between the masses in slavery here and freedom in Africa, is almost as great as the imaginative difference between the two future worlds of the Bible. The difference is the fruit of slavery. By the fruit the tree should be judged.

The seven years' famine which was the occasion of exalting Joseph to the control of Egypt, brought his father Jacob, and Jacob's other eleven sons, into the same kingdom, that they might avoid starvation by famine in the land of Canaan. A beautiful and productive portion of the land was assigned to them by the King. Here they became a nation, (Deut. ix. 34:) and enjoyed great prosperity and courtly favor for a long time; but at length a new King arose who knew nothing of Joseph.

The rapid increase of Jacob's posterity in Egypt awakened the fears of the new King, and he subjected them as a nation to bondage, and their male children to death. Now, let my reader remember that this was not domestic bondage, for they were the owners of domestic slaves themselves; they were literally a slaveholding nation, and so remained until their exodus. While they were compelled by Pharaoh to support themselves and their families—as their political master, he made very heavy drafts upon them for labor, and subjected them to unreasonable and cruel oppression by overtaxing their physical energies. This, we are told, was grievous to be borne, yet it "yielded the peaceable fruits of righteousness to them when exercised thereby." It led these slaveholders to call upon the Lord, in singleness of heart, for deliverance. The Lord heard their prayer, and delivered them from this cruel oppression—not, however, as modern deliverers seek deliverance for domestic slaves who are not oppressed; that is, by spears, Sharpe's rifles, conflagration, rapine and plunder. The lesson God taught this people by Moses is the lesson he teaches us by the Gospel; that is, that inflicting vengeance upon nations belongs to God—that we are not to avenge ourselves. These oppressed national bondmen peaceably petitioned the throne, under God's direction, for a release; and after the Almighty had endorsed their petitions by national judgments on Pharaoh, they were allowed to march peaceably out of Egypt with the consent of Pharaoh, their national master, carrying their own domestic slaves with them, without having received the permission of God individually, or as a nation, to perpetrate a deed of violence, or to offer an indignity to Pharaoh, or to any of their national oppressors. How does this comport with plans and efforts to release our domestic slaves who have no oppression to complain of? The domestic slaves of the Jews in Egypt had none to complain of. The oppressed in Egypt were masters—their bondage was political; from this God delivered them, and they marched peaceably, as a nation, to the Red Sea. Pharaoh pursued them—and here God destroyed him for a breach of his covenant to let them go. They marched through the Red Sea, as on dry land, and soon stood at the base of Mt. Sinai, where they received a moral constitution from the mouth of God himself; and soon after, through Moses, the laws ordaining and regulating, according to God's will, their system of domestic slavery, and their civil, social, and religious institutions. Here we see the Almighty displaying his vengeance upon the political oppressors of a nation of domestic slaveholders, while he writes his approval of their domestic slavery, by giving their slaves a place at the table of the passover the night these masters were delivered from political bondage, and their slaves at the same moment from the destroying angel for their masters' sake.

Their genealogies were carefully examined, and the male descendants of Abraham through Jacob, who could prove their descent, were formally recognized and reorganized as the nation to whom God had promised the land of Canaan. They numbered six hundred thousand fighting men. See Num. i. This nation voluntarily accepted the covenant God made with their fathers, and promised obedience to it. Exo. xix. 1 to 8.

The night they left Egypt the passover was instituted. It was to be a memorial of their national deliverance. The qualifications for its recipients are carefully worded in Exo. xii. 43, 44, 45. "A foreigner and an hired servant shall not eat thereof; but every man's servant that is bought for money, when thou hast circumcised him, then shall he eat thereof." This law proves Jacob's descendants to have been a nation of slaveholders when they left Egypt. They had been a slaveholding people during all the intervening time, from Abraham's day until they went down into Egypt with their father Jacob during the seven years of famine. This covers a period of more than four hundred and fifty years. Among the patriarchs of this period, their slaves are declared in the Bible to be, "their money;" they had bought them with their money, or they raised them in their families—and they were heritable property in perpetuity. Levit. xxv. 6. Slaves were carefully distinguished from hired servants and free men. And in the moral law, or ten commandments, delivered in less than three months after they left Egypt, their slaves are registered by the Almighty in the tenth commandment as their property, in common with other articles of property which were not to be coveted. See Exo. xx. 17. And in the fourth of the ten commandments rest from labor on the Sabbath was secured to these slaves. Exo. xx. 10. And now I ask again, how can any man who puts forth claims to Bible knowledge, solemnly declare and teach the world to believe, that the Bible makes slavery to be the greatest of all sins? Here is a miraculous interposition to deliver a nation of domestic slaveholders from a state of national bondage to which they had been subjected in Egypt. Can we believe God would do this, and sanction their holding slaves, if slavery was a great sin?

It may seem strange to an abolitionist (for they appear not to know what is in the Bible) that the Almighty should pollute His lips, in the blaze of glory that surrounded him, (at the time He proclaimed the ten commandments,) by acknowledging and legalizing a relation among men, that makes property of a fellow-being. They profess to believe this to be the greatest of sins. But their surprise will not be lessened when they discover, that in the next breath after enunciating the moral law, or ten commandments, the God of Abraham commences to deliver a body of law for the Jewish nation, the very first utterance of which enlarges the field in which they might lawfully secure a greater supply of slave labor.

The abolitionists of our day have been laboring to dry up the sources of supply; but the Almighty, in the first utterance of the law designed for the organization and regulation of their social and peculiar institutions, enlarges the boundary in which they may obtain a greater supply of slave labor. And in so doing has furnished the world a lesson for their instruction. They ought to study it.

For more than five hundred years Abraham's descendants had been domestic slaveholders; but until this time the Almighty had never given them his sanction to enslave their own brethren, and to make property of them. But He now opens a new source of supply for slave labor in several classes of Abraham's descendants. In the first place, He authorized Abraham's poor female children to be sold into hereditary bondage by their fathers. The proof of this is found in Exo. xxi. 7, and Deut. xv. 17. "If a man sell his daughter to be a maid servant, she shall not go out, as the men servants do." Again: He authorized the poor male descendants of Abraham to sell themselves and their wives into perpetual bondage. See Deut. xv. 12 to 17. And He allowed Abraham's male descendants when poor to be sold, or to sell themselves, their wives, and their children, into bondage for six years. If they had no wife when they were sold, then the Almighty allowed their master to give them one of his slave women to be their wife. If, at the end of six years, the man who came in with a wife and children chose to re-assume freedom, then he with his wife and children were entitled to it; and also to a provision made by the same law, *for* housekeeping again.

But in the case of him who had married his master's slave, she and her children remained the property of the master. If either of these men, after an experience of six years in slavery, preferred hereditary bondage to freedom, then the Almighty allowed them to alienate their freedom, and become slaves forever. Exo. xxi. 2 to 6. "If thou buy an Hebrew servant, six years he shall serve; and in the seventh he shall go out free for nothing. If he came in by himself, he shall go out by himself; if he were married, then his wife shall go out with him. If his master have given him a wife, and she have borne him sons or daughters, the wife and her children shall be her master's, and he shall go out by himself;" (and in Deut. xv. 13, 14, 18, the master is bound to furnish him for housekeeping again.) "But if the servant shall plainly say, I love my master, my wife, and my children; I will not go out free; then his master shall bring him unto the judges; he shall also bring him to the door, or unto the doorpost; and his master shall bore his ears through with an awl; and he shall serve him forever."

These persons belonged to classes, which will be found in all civilized society until time ends. The persons who make up these classes, embody moral purity in the outset of life; but are without the qualifications to contend successfully with the difficulties of securing a comfortable support —and hence they are exposed to the temptations which assail social virtue and moral purity with great severity. For the social comfort and moral security of these classes of his peculiar people, these laws were enacted by the Almighty.

There were other classes among Abraham's seed, that were subjected to slavery. These classes, also, have been found in civilized society in all ages and countries. They are criminal classes. For the good of these criminals whose punishment was short of death, and for the good of society, no human legislation has ever equalled the law of God. The classes he designed to correct by this legislation, included such persons as broke into houses—that stole cattle, sheep, or other stock—that trespassed on their neighbors' fields or forests—that appropriated to their own use whatever they could stealthily get hold of—that swindled by false pretences—that contracted debts without the means, or intention of paying them—in short, all who proved themselves unfit to be trusted with freedom.

The object to be accomplished by these laws was to dry up the sources of moral miasma; neutralize this poison; improve the morals of the culprits, and preserve the health of the social body. One great principle lies at the bottom of all this legislation, which was enacted of God to relieve society—first, of criminals; secondly, to correct the criminal classes—and third, to save the virtuous poor from that condition of poverty which leads to crime. This great principle, the abolitionists say, is the very essence of sin. It is the principle which makes the service, or labor of a human being, to be money or property. By the aid of this principle, labor was made a legal tender in the payment of debts—it was declared to be money, and by this money the Almighty secured in the first place, for the poor female children of Abraham's sons, social equality in good families, and a good home for life. Their master was authorized to marry them himself, or to marry them to his sons, or to any male descendant of Abraham; thus, poor female children were shielded by their masters from vice, and were made valuable contributors to the general welfare.

The owners of capital thus secured by the law, in buying the female labor for life, would give their capital a form for the profitable employment of such labor—and that to an extent, that would equal the supply of it. Thus, their cities would not become Sodoms. And thus, from poor young females—the most demoralizing of all classes in exclusive freedom, a healthy tone would be given to society, and a supply of female labor secured for the spindle and distaff, to meet the demands of taste, and to supply the comforts of life. How different is such a result from that of capital employed in some of our northern cities; where it is used to secure and furnish from one to one hundred or more rooms, into which these poor females can be seduced to enter, that they may secure a return for the capital of their employer, by a course of conduct which leaves the community a Sodom—emasculated of virtue, and a moral stench upon the face of the earth. Ten thousand of these poor innocents, it is said, are thus sacrificed annually in one single northern city in our Union. From thence they are shipped like merchandise to every place where a market can be found. They are compelled annually to give place to a new supply. To subject them to domestic slavery in good families—to render them useful to society—to give them in marriage to raise families —and thus to preserve the moral health and social happiness of the community, would be the greatest of sins, according to the morals and political standard of the abolitionists.

In the second place, the poor man and his wife, unable from the want of skill to succeed against competition, were allowed of God to throw off all anxious care, to sit down in social quietude, and to enjoy the provision secured by labor to domestic bondmen for life. The innocent poor thus provided for, the future danger to society thus guarded against—the Almighty, by the aid of this great money principle, next subjected the criminal classes to a more efficient remedy, and society to a less costly correction, than that of building penitentiaries and workhouses, and employing incompetent overseers at high wages to look over these criminals, whose moral renovation could not be expected as a result from their condition. Instead of such an agency, He subjected them to the control of domestic masters, who were interested in their labor and deportment, and who could use magisterial authority at pleasure for the correction of all insubordination. Upon crime he placed a very high money price. For a few stolen articles the prices to be paid by the criminal are specified: for an ox, the price of five oxen, &c. These specifications were the basis of a general principle, by which the judges were to be governed in the punishment of offences not specified. This money, when the criminal was poor, was raised by the sale of his labor, and was to pay the injured party for his loss, and the State for her expense. To raise this money the State sold the culprit's service or labor, and passed to the purchaser a right to control him by all necessary and proper means. These means the State furnished when necessary.

By this system of making labor a merchantable commodity, the productive resources of the State were increased, the personal and property rights of the people were secured, prolific sources of vice and crime were dried up, and the morals of the community preserved and strengthened. But, according to the abolition standard of morals and unalienable rights, God must be the greatest sinner in the universe if he be the author of such laws as the above. John Brown is eulogized as a martyr for resisting to the death such laws as I have quoted, or referred to from the Bible. He left many behind him, who are boiling with rage against all such enactments.

I will now pass by these laws of the Almighty for a supply of slave labor among Abraham's seed, where it had never before been furnished, to the law of God, which opens the markets of the world to his descendants, in quest of this labor. He tells them in Levit. xxv. 44, 45: "Both thy bondmen and thy bondmaids, which thou shalt have, shall be of the heathen that are round about you; of them shall ye buy bondmen and bondmaids. Moreover, of the children of the strangers that do sojourn among you, of them shall ye buy, and of their families that are with you which they begat in your land: and they shall be your possession. And ye shall take them as an inheritance for your children after you to inherit them for a possession: they shall be your bondmen forever." By this law the markets of the nations in all directions were opened of God for the purchase of slaves by Abraham's seed; except the seven nations of Canaan. These seven nations were to be entirely destroyed without mercy by God's command, in Deut. xx. 16, 17. "But of the cities of these people, which the Lord thy God doth give thee for an inheritance, thou shalt save alive nothing that breatheth. But thou shalt utterly destroy them, namely: the Hittites, and the Amorites; the Canaanites, and the Perrizites; the Hivites, and the Jebusites; as the Lord thy God hath commanded thee." And again, in Deut. vii. 2, they are commanded "to make no covenant with them, nor show mercy unto them."

The law which opened to the Israelites all the national markets around them, does not stop until it gives them the divine sanction to purchase slaves of all the strangers who might choose to dwell among them. These strangers loved the Israelites, and therefore followed them from Egypt. These strangers shared largely in the Divine favor. Three several times the Israelites are commanded not "to vex or oppress them; but to love them as themselves." Exo. xxii. 21; Levit. xix. 33, 34; Deut. xxiv. 14. Yet God allows the Israelites to buy and hold these strangers in hereditary bondage, as an inheritance to their children forever. Here is *proof positive*, without interference, that to *buy* and *hold* a person *in slavery*, harmonizes with *loving that person as ourself*. God *commands* the Israelites to *love these strangers as themselves*, and at the *same time authorizes* them *to buy* and *hold them as slaves*.

Can any right-minded man survey these great facts of the Bible and then bring himself to believe that slavery is sinful; or, that it is not in harmony with God's moral perfections, or the obligation He has laid on men to love each other? Freedom was a curse to the lawless portion of Abraham's seed. Their freedom was a curse also to the State, and therefore God directed the State to take it from them, and subject them to slavery.

Freedom to Abraham's poor and exposed female children, seems also to have been a curse to them and the community; God, therefore, in mercy to them and the State, allowed their parents to invest them with the advantages of domestic slavery. To Abraham's male descendants who had families, without the skill to provide for them, He extended the same advantages.

All these classes were benefited by slavery. The idolatrous class was better governed, better protected, better fed and clothed, better instructed for this life and that to come, shared in social sympathy and intelligence, unknown to them in heathenism, and were greatly favored by the Almighty in allowing them to stand in such a relation to a people whose God was the eternal I AM. And does not truth compel us to say all this of the African race on this continent? These Africans were the most degraded, superstitious, and ignorant of all the heathen races on earth. By domestic slavery they have been brought into a progressive state of civilization, and to share largely in the blessings of the Gospel.

The Almighty, in the law which sanctioned slavery, guarded the slave against cruelty and limited the master's discretion to the use of necessary and proper means for controlling his slave. For cruelty, the master was responsible, and the slave was released from bondage. The laws of God for the government and protection of freemen and slaves, furnish a very instructive lesson to all honest-minded men who reverence the Bible, in ascertaining the truth of the infidel doctrine, that all men are born free and equal. For the benefit of such well-meaning men, I will quote a few of these laws: If a man maimed his own slave, by knocking out his eye, or his tooth, the slave was to be freed, as a punishment upon the master for this wanton act of personal violence, which was neither proper nor necessary, as a means of securing subordination. Exo. xxi. 26, 27. But for the same offence committed against a free person, the offender had to pay an eye for an eye, and a tooth for a tooth, as the penalty. Levit. xxiv. 19, 20. Question: Will these two laws carry the idea of freedom and equality to an honest mind? Again. If a slave lost his life by an ox running at large, and known by the owner of the ox to be dangerous, the owner of the ox had to pay thirty shekels of silver to the master, as a compensation for the loss of his slave. Exo. xxi. 32. But if the person so killed was free, then the owner forfeited his life. Exo. xxi. 29. Question: Do these two laws of the Almighty teach the freedom and equality of modern infidelity? Again. Under the law of God the male descendants of Abraham were allowed to marry slave women. If under this law a man married his own slave, his children by her were free; but if he married the slave of another man, his children by her were the slaves of her owner. Exo. xxi. 1–4. By this law, we see that a free man's children may be born hereditary slaves. Question: What support do we get here for the infidel doctrine, "that all men are born free and equal." Again. Under this law, if a slave woman was engaged to be married to a free man—for unfaithfulness, she was subjected to stripes, and her seducer to the penalty of a sheep, as a sacrifice for sin. Levit. xix. 20 to 22. But for the same offence, a free woman and her seducer forfeited their lives. Deut. xxi. 23, 24. Question: Can any man feel as much justified by the Bible in believing all men are born free and equal, as I feel in furnishing him with the means, and then requesting him to use them for the correction of his error?

This body of slave law was in force among Abraham's seed until the coming of Christ—a period of fifteen hundred years. During this long period they disobeyed the Almighty in a great many ways. His judgments were sent upon them for their disobedience. These judgments were inflicted for causes that are on record in the Old Testament. Before inflicting these judgments, the Almighty raised up prophets to make known to them their sins,—to warn them of their danger,—and to exhort them to repentance. In all the indictments filed against them by the prophets, there is not one for holding slaves in bondage. The law authorized them to hold their brethren in bondage for six years, and it authorized them to hold the heathen in bondage forever. It required them at the end of the six years to restore their Hebrew brethren to freedom again. For the violation of this last law, which required them to restore their Hebrew brethren to freedom again at the end of six years, the prophet Jeremiah was sent to them with this message: "Thus, saith the Lord, the God of Israel, I made a covenant with your fathers in the day that I brought them forth out of the land of Egypt, out of the house of bondmen, saying, At the end of seven years let ye go every man his brother, an Hebrew which hath been sold unto thee, and when he hath served thee six years, thou shalt let him go free from thee: but your fathers hearkened not unto me, neither inclined their ear; therefore, thus saith the Lord, Ye have not hearkened unto me in proclaiming liberty every one to his brother, and every man to his neighbor; behold, I proclaim a liberty to you, saith the Lord, to the sword, to the pestilence, and to the famine, and I will make you to be removed into all the kingdoms of the earth." This judgment was sent upon them for violating the law which authorized them to enslave their Hebrew brethren for six years, written in Exo. xxi. 2. The judgment pronounced against them by Jeremiah, the prophet, for violating this law, will be found in Jer. xxxiv. 13 to 17.

In Levit. xix. 13, the law for the wages of free labor declares: "The wages of him that is hired shall not abide with thee all night until the morning." For the violation of this law the Lord proclaimed this judgment by the mouth of Jeremiah against Jehoiakim, son of Josiah, king of Judah: "Woe unto him that buildeth his house by unrighteousness, and his chambers by wrong; that useth his neighbor's service without wages," (not his slave's service without wages, but his neighbor's service without wages,) "and giveth him not for his work; that saith, I will build me a wide house, and large chambers, and cutteth him out windows; and it is ceiled with cedar, and painted with vermilion. Shalt thou reign because thou closest thyself in cedar? Did not thy father eat and drink, and do judgment and justice, and then it was well with him? He judged the cause of the poor and needy;" (to see that their wages were paid to them;) "then it was well with him: was not this to know me, saith the Lord? But thine eyes and thine heart are not but for thy covetousness and for oppression and violence *to do it*. Therefore, thus saith the Lord, concerning Jehoiakim, They shall not lament for him, he shall be buried with the burial of an ass, drawn and cast forth beyond the gates of Jerusalem." Jer. xxii. 13 to 19, inclusive.

The oppression of the hireling, in not having his wages paid to him, is one of the great sins of the Old Testament. The abolitionists gather up all the passages in which this sin of oppression is spoken of, and apply the sin to Southern slaveholders. They profess to believe that the slave of the South is defrauded of wages for his labor; to which, according to the Bible, he is entitled as a hireling; overlooking, at the same time, the astonishing and remarkable fact, that, as a class, they receive wages in the shape of a comfortable home for life, and a supply for their wants that is equalled by no such number of free laborers on the globe.

For the benefit of men, who wish to know the truth of the Bible on this subject, I will add a little for their instruction. In the first place, the hireling of the Bible, who is not to be oppressed, and whose oppression is the great sin of the Bible, is the free man of the Bible, or the man whom the Bible declares to be free—and not the hereditary bondman of the Bible, the man who is declared by the Bible to be his master's money. All this will be seen in the legislative protection given by the law of Moses to three classes of laborers. These three different classes of laborers are plainly set forth in that law. Two of these classes were created by that law—the other class by their own free choice. The two classes created by the law were slaves—the other class consisted of free persons, who hired themselves to work for wages. One of these slave classes were Abraham's descendants, who were sold under the sanction of the law into slavery for six years. At the end of this time they were released by the law from this slavery, and restored to their freedom again The other class of these slaves were heathens, who were bought for money according to the law in xxv. Leviticus, and were made by that law to be their masters' money, and to be hereditary bondmen and bondwomen to him and his children forever.

For the class of free laborers who hired themselves for wages, a law was enacted, (which has been quoted,) that required their wages to be paid to them promptly. For the violation of this law God threatened to visit, not the employer only, but the whole nation with severe judgments—thereby making all the individuals of the nation responsible for the due execution of this law. For the violation of this law, King Jehoiakim and the nation were visited with the awful judgment I have previously stated from Jer. xxii. 13, 19.

For the protection of Abraham's seed, who were in bondage for six years, a law was passed which exempted them in the first place from the rigorous treatment of heathen slaves, Levit. xxv. 39 to 43, and restored them in the second place to freedom again at the end of the six years. For a violation of this latter section of the law, God threatened the whole nation with judgments, thereby making the nation, as well as the master, responsible for retaining Abraham's seed in bondage beyond the six years, except in cases where they voluntarily chose to subject themselves to hereditary bondage, after the six years were ended. This law, as I have before stated, was violated by Zedekiah, king of Judah, and by others through his example. For this sin the nation was overthrown, Jerusalem destroyed, Zedekiah's sons and nobles slain before his eyes, Zedekiah's eyes put out, and he bound in chains to be carried to Babylon by the Chaldeans.

Nothing is more prominent in the Old Testament than the legal protection given to free labor. God threatened by judgments, that were awful, to avenge the oppressions of the free laborer. There is one law for their benefit, which embodies the divine benevolence in a very conspicuous manner. He gives the free laborer a right to borrow of his brother, (even victuals when hard pressed,) and makes it the duty of that rich brother, under a heavy penalty—that of having God's blessing withheld—to loan him a supply, and that without usury, and to release him from all that was unpaid at the Sabbatic year, or the year of release. Deut. xv. 7 to 10. The Divine legislation for this class of free laborers suggests to the mind that there is a natural tendency with the rich to oppress free labor—because, in all God's legislation against oppression, there is not a law passed, or a judgment threatened to guard the hereditary slave against want, or oppression of any kind, save that of personal abuse in anger. To prevent this, he freed the slave so treated, as we have seen in Exo. xx. 26, 27. This remarkable fact of legislative silence for the protection of slaves, can only be accounted for by supposing, what we of the South know to be true, that the relation of master and slave, which God ordained between the superior races of Shem and Japheth and the inferior race of Ham, was a relation that in the nature of things constituted the strongest guarantee, which can bind the superior to take care of the inferior man. That it was more effectual than legal enactments enforced by the severest penalties—and therefore no laws were necessary to secure the hereditary slave from oppression and want, as the relation itself would make it the interest of the master to provide well for his slave, and not oppress him. This relation abates "the irrepressible conflict" between free labor and capital, and secures the affection and confidence of the slave to his master and family where he lacks nothing. And hence the remarkable fact, that in all the divine legislation for a slaveholding nation there is not a single law, express or implied, against servile insurrection. The wisdom of this omission is proved by the historical fact, that, in the fifteen hundred years of their national existence, they never had a single fear awakened on that subject.

Their various wars, and the awful calamities and burdens of their wars, fell upon men who were free—while their domestic slaves were sitting under their vines and fig-trees in peace. For the privileges and blessings of slavery under such circumstances, the Jews themselves, in the wilderness, often turned back in their hearts, greatly preferring their slavery among the flesh-pots, onions, and leeks of Egypt, to the perils, dangers, and privations of freedom—as you will see by reading their history during their forty years' sojourn in the wilderness.

Their history further proves that, after they were quietly settled in their own land, there was an irrepressible conflict between free labor and capital, or between the rich and the poor. This began to show itself with the oppressions of King Saul; and was intensified until the oppressions and exactions of King Solomon upon free labor led, just after his death, to civil war and disunion—ten tribes on the one side, and two on the other, arrayed in bitter hostility and deadly strife, until the names of the ten tribes were blotted out from the catalogue of nations. This conflict between free labor and capital will always be greater or less, according to the law of supply and demand; that is, when the supply of free labor is large, and the demand for it small—the price of labor comes down below the laborer's necessary wants, and he is rendered desperate in his feelings towards the owners of capital. On the other hand, when the demand for free labor is greater than the supply of it, then the laborer extorts a price for it beyond its value, and then men of capital become desperate in their turn and meditate revenge. This antagonism and its consequent alienation can only be prevented by a controlling sense of justice.

When our Northern brethren get their consent in years of difficulty and small profits, to share with free labor the profits of prosperous years—as we find it our interest as well as pleasure to do with our slaves at the South, they will abate this irrepressible conflict among them; which already needs every now and then the strong arm of the government to suppress it—and which, if not checked by a nearer approach to justice, will bring forth the fruit it has always produced—that of some bold spirit, who, like Jeroboam, will seize the sword and put an end to anarchy by burying, in the grave of despotism, the liberty and the covetousness of wealth which produced it.

I will now leave the Old Testament and open the New, to see what our Saviour and the apostles did with slavery. Rome swayed her sceptre at the time over one hundred and twenty millions of people. According to a most careful survey, not of translations, but of all the ancient authorities in the original languages in which they were written, Gibbon affirms that one-half of these one hundred and twenty millions were domestic slaves; that they were made slaves by victory over opposing nations; that the enslaved were persons of every rank; that the means of controlling them was left to the discretion of the master; that the power of life and death, without responsibility to the State, was in his hands; that this was the state of things in the Roman empire, when the missionaries of the Cross were sent through that empire and the world to set up the Kingdom of Christ.

Now the question to be settled is this, What did Christ and the apostles do with slavery? They were obliged to meet with it everywhere. It existed everywhere—among Jews and Gentiles. The first thing done by Christ in person, in reference to this and all other subjects of like kind, was to disclose and act out one great principle. That principle was, that earthly governments were ordained of God for the regulation of human conduct in all the relations of this life, and that these governments were to be obeyed and honored, and that our spiritual relations to God involved no obligations to disobey them.

This line of separation which gives to God only jurisdiction under the first table of the law, and which gives to man jurisdiction only under the second table of the law, was disclosed in the Saviour's reply to the Pharisees. They supposed, if he had courage to speak the truth, he would have proclaimed to Abraham's seed exemption from obedience to the law of the Roman empire. The law of Moses was from God. The Roman law was from sinful man. The Pharisees thought that disobedience to Cæsar was obedience to God. This was John Brown's theory. It is the theory of all the fanatics at the North. The Saviour's doctrine is contained in his reply to the Pharisees. That reply is in these words: "Render unto Cæsar the things that are Cæsar's, and unto God the things that are God's." The same doctrine is taught by him when tribute was wrongfully demanded of him at the Sea of Galilee. He thought on that occasion and acted out the principle, that submission to earthly governments was a duty, even when in our private judgments its power was abused, as was the case in that instance, in exacting of him, a Jew, what strangers only were bound to pay. That the lesson might be more impressive, he refused to be released from personal responsibility, and sent Peter to get tribute money for them both from the mouth of a fish, which he made to serve him on the occasion, by an exercise of his divine power. Refusing to acknowledge this principle and to act upon it, cost John Brown his life. Before Pilate our Saviour proclaimed the same great principle when he said, "My kingdom is not of this world;" meaning thereby that allegiance to God in religion involved no treason, but obedience, to earthly governments; if otherwise, twelve legions of angels would have lent him their aid to overthrow them. Brown differed with the Saviour; he thought obedience to government wrong, and treason against government right; for his wickedness he lost his life.

Although Christ was a king, and had a kingdom here on earth; yet it was not set up for worldly purposes—it was not to wage war upon the governments of the world. Its sphere of operation and supremacy was the heart of man. Its design was to call into exercise the spirit of good-will to man and peace on earth. Christ taught that the subjects of his kingdom were still to retain the civil and political relations they had previously held to earthly governments. The husband, the wife, the parent, the child, the master, the servant, the ruler and the people, when called by grace into his kingdom, were to abide in these relations, and were still bound to render obedience to their respective earthly governments, and that, in doing so, they were rendering obedience to God as well as to man.

There is perfect harmony between the teachings of Christ on this subject before his death, and the teachings of the apostles after his ascension to heaven. On the subject of submission and obedience to earthly government by the followers of Christ, we have the following plain instruction by the Apostle Paul to the Church, (or rather the churches, for there were several of them,) planted in the city of Rome. In the xiii. of his letter to these churches, some of whose members belonged to Cæsar's household, from the 1st to the 8th verses he says: "Let every soul be subject to the higher powers: the powers that be, are ordained of God. Whosoever, therefore, resisteth the power resisteth the ordinance of God: and they that resist shall receive to themselves damnation. Wilt thou then not be afraid of the power? Do that which is good and thou shalt have praise of the same; for he is the minister of God to thee for good. But if thou do that which is evil, be afraid; for he beareth not the sword in vain; for he is the minister of God; a revenger, to execute wrath upon him that doeth evil. Wherefore ye must needs be subject, not only for wrath, but also for conscience sake. For, for this cause pay ye tribute also; for they are God's ministers, attending continually on this very thing. Render therefore to all their dues; tribute to whom tribute is due; custom to whom custom; fear to whom fear; honor to whom honor."

Here is the political creed of Jesus Christ; delivered by the Apostle Paul to all Christians. Comment on this creed to make it plainer, would be like gilding pure gold. The apostle here teaches that human governments are God's ordinances, that they originate in his will, that he has delegated to them his authority to punish evil doers, and that Christian obedience to human governments is service done to God.

The government within whose limits this subjection and obedience would be first called into exercise, was a government that sanctioned slavery. It was a government, as we have seen, that sanctioned the use of all such means in securing the subordination of the slave, as the master in his discretion might think proper to use. This obedience to civil government is enjoined, not only to avoid wrath, or the penalty of the law, which is God's wrath but this obedience was to be rendered for conscience sake towards God. How great must be the difference between such a conscience and that of the "higher law!" One of these consciences, made by the political creed of Christ, presents an offering to God *of the obedience* it has rendered to human government as service done to him. The other of these consciences, made by the "higher law," presents an offering to God of the *rebellion and treason* it has made against human government as service done to him. Are both of these offerings alike acceptable in the sight of God? Who will answer, yea?

It may be that some will ask, Does Christ sanction, as right, all the abuses of power in human governments? Not at all. He commands all that is right, and sanctions nothing wrong in his kingdom, and leaves all other kingdoms to the control of those who are providentially responsible to him for the exercise of their authority in civil matters. His kingdom, which is not of this world, was intended to be the "light of the world." His kingdom is "righteousness and peace." Every subject of his kingdom is required, if it be possible, "to live peaceably with all men," and to "seek after the things that make for peace." When his kingdom reflects "righteousness, peace on earth and good-will to man," it puts forth all its legitimate power for the correction of wrong in earthly kingdoms. When the professed subjects of his kingdom take the sword, not as a citizen in obedience to civil authority, but as Christians in obedience to Christ, to resist human governments as Peter did, when he struck off the ear of the law-officer, the Saviour admonishes them that they shall perish by the sword.

The Apostle Peter gives the political creed of Jesus Christ to all Christians, in the following words: "Submit yourselves to every ordinance of man for the Lord's sake, whether it be to the king as supreme, or unto governors, as unto them that are appointed by him, for so is the will of God. Honor all men; love the brotherhood; fear God; honor the king. Servants, be subject to your masters; wives, submit yourselves to your husbands; husbands, dwell with them, according to knowledge; giving honor to the wife. Finally, do not render evil for evil, but blessing; don't return railing for railing; refrain the tongue from evil, and the lips from guile; eschew evil; do good; seek peace, and ensue it. But, and if ye suffer when ye do all these, how then?" Well, says the apostle, "if when ye do well and suffer for it, ye take it patiently, this is acceptable with God; for even hereunto were ye called."

Here we see the case supposed, that after rendering the most perfect political fidelity to government, yet Christians may be called to suffer by an abuse of political power. Instead, however, of releasing Christians from allegiance to government in such cases, or authorizing wholesale murder and treason by men who had never been called to suffer at all; the apostle teaches that this suffering on the part of Christians for patient continuance in well doing, is acceptable with God, and that they are hereunto called by him. 1 Peter ii. 13 to 25.

From this plain instruction, given for the government of Chistians in their political relations, what are we to think of the "higher law" crusade of the present day, made, not by citizens in obedience to any authority recognized of God, but professedly in the name and to meet the demands of Christ, whose "kingdom is not of this world?"

Again: The Apostle Paul, in writing a letter to Titus, who was an evangelist, shows a special solicitude that Christians should be taught by him the great duty of submission to earthly governments, and that they should not be allowed to *forget their duty in this behalf.* Hence the re-

3

markable language in Titus iii. 1, 2: "*put them in mind* to be subject to principalities and powers, to obey magistrates, to be ready for every good work, to speak evil of no man, to be no brawlers, but gentle, showing all meekness to all men."

Again, the same solicitude is shown by the same apostle in writing a letter to Timothy. Timothy and Titus were evangelists, employed by the apostle in visiting the churches, and preaching the Gospel on each side of the maritime boundary which separates Europe from Asia, and from thence eastward and westward along the continents of Asia and Europe, and among the islands of the Mediterranean Sea, from Rome down to the borders of Arabia. In this first letter of Paul to Timothy, ii. 1, 2, he exhorts him to instruct the churches, that, in exhibiting the character of Christianity in its doctrines, spirit, and *practical requirements*, they let their loyalty to earthly governments be very conspicuous. First of all, he exhorts Timothy, and all the members, to let rulers and all in authority, and all who attended their worship, know the solicitude Christians felt for the honor and success of their rulers, as the ministers of God, into whose hands he had committed the welfare of the State.

Having shown, as I trust, by the example and teaching of Christ—and by the teaching of the apostles, that governments such as then existed, (and they are known to have been slaveholding,) are declared by the apostles to be ordinances of God, and that obedience to them is one of the highest earthly duties enjoined upon Christians, I will now proceed to show that the relation of slavery sought to be overthrown by our Northern brethren is not only not condemned as a sin, nor prohibited by the Bible, but fully sanctioned as a lawful relation among men by Christ and his apostles.

CHAPTER III.

A General View of what the Bible teaches on Slavery until the Ascension of Christ—Paul to the Gentiles—His Ephesian Letter—Spiritualism—Idolatry—Abolitionism—Forbids fellowship with Abolitionists—His Letter to Timothy—To Titus—To Corinth—Peter's Letter to the Jews—Authority given the Husband, the Father, the Master—Obedience enjoined upon the Wife, the Child, the Slave—The relation between the parties ordained by God—Based upon Justice—Reciprocal Duties—Obedience to God—Obedience, a test of Discipleship—The Teaching of the Apostles—The Teaching of the Abolitionists—One Godliness, the other Blasphemy—The Colossian Letter—Paul returns a Runaway Slave to his Master—The reason assigned—His example copied when the Federal Constitution was formed—Objections answered—Note.

It may be of service to my reader, if he is desirous to see this subject in the light of the Bible, to have a brief but connected view of it from the first ray of Bible light, which is shed upon it, until the New Testament is closed.

Slavery is first brought to view in connection with God's newly disclosed purpose, after the flood, of subdividing the descendants of Noah into nations. This purpose was effected by dividing their tongues or languages. Until the flood, Adam's descendants formed but one great family, speaking the same language, with political and social equality. The result was that the earth was soon filled wth violence. This was written for our learning, and it is full of instruction.

Noah had three sons, Shem, Ham, and Japheth. These three sons are declared by the Almighty to be types of the several nations that would descend from them. They are made typical representatives of superior, inferior, and medium nations. Their several localities were selected of God for each class of these nations to occupy on the globe, and their habitations were adapted to their type of character.

God announced his purpose of subordinating these nations one to another. This subordination was to harmonize with their leading traits of character, and its ultimate object was their general good. The character given of God to each of these three sons, is the character of their descendants at the present moment. Ham was enslaved of God to Shem and Japheth. The propriety of this was first seen in the abuse Ham's descendants made of freedom while they enjoyed it in the land of Canaan. From that day until this, their history proves that freedom to them is a curse, and not a blessing, and that Ham's character is a true type of the character of his descendants.

Shem is characterized as the subject of reverence for the true God, in the midst of idolatry and wickedness—and is a true type of his descendants through Abraham until the present hour. It was with Abraham and his descendants that his mission was inaugurated.

Shem was made the father of nations, whose mission was that of treasure-keepers and promulgators of the divine mind. His mission was organized in Abraham's family under the patriarchal form of government, and was re-organized in the wilderness when he entered, as a nation, upon his mission in the land of Canaan—which he prosecuted until the coming of Christ.

Ham, the inferior son, was subjected to slavery, and his mission involved an obligation to serve Shem, when Shem entered upon his mission in the land of Canaan. This, we have seen, they were made to do by the enactment of the Mosaic law.

Japheth, from small beginnings, was made to engirdle the globe. His mission involved the responsibility which attaches to universal dominion.

His first home, given him of God, was in the islands of the sea; but God promised to enlarge him in his geographical and intellectual dimensions, until he should not only occupy Europe, but dwell in the tents of Shem; or, in other words, until, by the influence which enterprising intelligence would give him, Shem would quietly defer to him throughout Asia. Asia was Shem's home.

Ham was devoted of God, not only to serve Shem, while Shem was prosecuting his mission in the land of Canaan, but he was devoted of God to serve Japheth also, while Japheth was prosecuting the great mission assigned of God to him, of developing the intellectual and material treasures of the entire globe.

Japheth's mission involved the obligation to promote the individual and general good of the whole human family. Ham was first to serve Shem in his mission, and then to serve Japheth in his mission. The substance of these views necessarily involves dominion for Japheth over Ham in all nations, and a controlling influence over Shem in Asia.

These prophetic paintings are to be found in Gen. ix. 19 to 27, and in x. Here we see the divine plan unfolded for controlling or governing all the subdivisions or social organizations among men. In this plan equality among nations, as well as individuals, is repudiated, and a subordination, that has reference to character and qualification, is established.

Ham is brought to our view in these and the subjoined inspired rays of light in the context, as the slave of shameless animal propensities—without self-respect, and is made the representative type of those nations, or individuals to descend from him, who, for their resemblance to him, should be subjected to the control of superiors for their own good, and that of the world. Shem appears in these rays of divine light, with characteristic reverence for the true God. This reverence always includes qualities which fit men to control the slaves of animal appetites, devoid of self-respect, and to train them in virtue and religion; hence Ham is made a slave, and subjected to Shem's control. Japheth is enlarged by the Almighty, until he dwells in Shem's tents, or, in other words, until he controls Asia. And he is further enlarged by the Almighty until Ham is made his servant, and he Ham's master—or, in other words, until he exercises despotic control over Ham, and friendly control over Shem, in working out the great results of human progress.

This shows that in God's plan for securing these results, in nations as well as in families, slavery must be used as a necessary means for controlling, improving, and elevating the inferior and degraded man. It shows also that qualifications, fitting men for religious progress, such as Shem had, are not the qualifications which fit them for political and scientific progress. This shows also that the medium man may do well in religion, while he cannot rise above mediocrity in the higher attainments of science and skill, in the progressive developments of the natural world, unless Japheth, or the superior man, will dwell in his tent and lead him on in the path of progress. Religious progress is best promoted by the moral power of the masses—the world's progress by the intellectual power of the classes.

The great truth of Japheth's superiority and mission has been in a course of development since he was inaugurated in the west of Europe. In China, the East Indies, and Asia generally, Shem had risen to a level above which he can never rise unaided. Ham never has shared, and probably never can, in the great results of Japheth's mission, without the absolute control of Japheth as a humane benefactor. Freedom and equality are Ham's social poison. Moral health or intellectual manhood cannot be secured to him while he drinks this poison.

Slavery was decreed of God for the correction of sin, and the good of the world. It made its appearance according to the Bible, first in the family of Abraham, in the domestic form. This took place when God called Abraham from Ur of the Chaldees, to inaugurate Shem's mission, under the patriarchal form of government. God called him into the land of Canaan to survey the theatre upon which, after four hundred years, his mission was to be prosecuted to its consummation, under a national form of government, with God himself as the lawgiver and governor. Abraham, while prosecuting his high trust of treasure-keeper and promulgator of God's will, bought and raised a very large family of slaves. At his death, this man who was selected of God to know and teach his will, gave these slaves to his son Isaac in perpetuity. Isaac, at his death, willed them to Jacob. Jacob, while young, married in Padan Aram, and by his own skill and industry made large additions, by purchase, to these slaves which he inherited at his father's death. With these slaves, and their increase in Egypt, Abraham's seed were miraculously led by the Almighty from Egypt to the land of Canaan. They had then been domestic slaveholders for some four hundred and fifty years. While the Almighty delivered them from national bondage, he fully sanctioned their system of domestic bondage, in allowing their slaves to celebrate the passover, and prohibiting it to hired servants. They were required, when they reached the promised land, to destroy utterly, without mercy, seven of the most degraded nations of Ham's descendants, and to enslave the balance of them; which amounted, at that time, to seven or eight nations more, within the limits given to Abraham by promise. God gave to Abraham's seed, at the same time, the markets of the world also, for a larger supply of slave labor; and authorized them to enslave poor young females of their own race, to save them from poverty and crime; and to enslave such of their own brothers with families, as had not skill to provide for themselves. They were directed, also, to subject their criminal brothers to the domestic control and service of masters, that their morals might be corrected, and society secured against their aggressions. All this shows that God's peculiar people were taught to use slavery as a good to the degraded and helpless. And it is written in the Scriptures for our learning.

When Shem's mission was ended in Asia by the coming of Christ, Japheth had begun in Europe to assume the responsibilities of his mission. It was at this time that the Saviour set up his kingdom. We are deeply interested, therefore, in knowing what Jesus did in his kingdom with slavery, which Japheth had established, within the limits of his control. His control, or government, extended over a hundred and twenty millions of souls.

We have already seen that Christ interfered in no way with the prerogatives of earthly government. But we have seen also, that within his own kingdom he exercised *absolute control over every thing sinful in the sight of God*, whether it be that which is sinful in itself, or that which is made to be sin by Divine prohibition. If slavery, therefore, be sinful in either of these respects, it must be prohibited in the Church of Christ; and just here, let me remark once for all, that if slavery be a lawful relation, yet it is a relation that subjects the slave very often to injustice and cruelty by the master, just as the marriage relation very often does the wife; just as the parental relation very often does the child; just as the political relation of ruler and people very often does the subject. The authority given of God in all these relations is often abused by those who exercise it. Now, let it be noticed by my reader, that Christ, in his kingdom, has given his full sanction and approval to all those relations, but not to their abuse. And let my reader notice, that Christ, in his kingdom, has corrected all the abuses of authority in these several relations; and has made obedience in them, to be obedience to God; requiring that this obedience be rendered with good will to the authoritative head of these relations. This is as true of all these relations, as it is of any one of them.

The reasoning which aims to destroy the relation of slavery, because of injustice, cruelty, or oppression on the part of the master, will apply with exactly the same force against the marriage relation, the paternal relation, and that of ruler and people, because God's authority in all these relations can be abused—and his authority in all of them is abused. If, therefore, the abuse of his authority in one of them makes the relation to be sinful, then the abuse of his authority in the others, makes them to be sinful also: In the Church of Christ, the abuse of God's authority in these relations is prohibited, and the right use of his authority is enjoined. It is enjoined equally in all, as in any one of them.

While abolitionism holds slavery to be a sin, yet it admits it was sanctioned in the Church. If this be so, then, according to abolitionism, the direction given to masters and slaves in the New Testament, is direction given to teach them how to live in sin; and so of the direction given to husband and wife, parent and child, ruler and people. Consistency will make all these directions, to be directions given to the parties to teach them how to live in sin. How can we establish a difference when the Holy Ghost has made no difference? God, in his word, has established each relation, and given to its head the authority to govern. He has enjoined obedience in all these relations, and for the same end in all. That is, that God may be glorified—as you will see in the references now to be made.

The object now to be accomplished, is simply to show from the New Testament that the Roman slavery which existed when the Gospel was first proclaimed, was a relation which the Gospel sanctioned as lawful, and that its reciprocal duties, enjoined upon the master and the servant, grow out of the relation itself; that they do not exist outside of it, and that they rest upon the foundation of justice, just as do the duties of husband and wife, parent and child, ruler and people. These relations all involve justice. The duty enjoined upon the husband gives him a just right to the obedience of his wife. This duty of the husband is an equivalent for the obedience of the wife, and that rendered in the best form. The performance of the duty enjoined upon the wife, gives her a just right to all that God has enjoined upon the husband; and so of master and slave, parent and child, ruler and people. Those duties which God enjoins upon the master, give him a just right to the service or labor of his slave; and that service or labor gives the slave a just right to all which God has commanded the master to render for it; and so of parent and child, ruler and people. Authority and control are given on one side, obedience and service are enjoined on the other. These are all relations of justice, because that which is rendered by one side is justly paid for by an equivalent on the other. These reciprocal duties grow out of the relation itself. They are based upon justice, and are not due where the relation does not exist.

The legality of slavery in the sight of God is proved by the inspired and authoritative letters of the apostles. These letters were written to organized Gospel churches. They were written for the purpose of teaching those churches, and all others through them, what the Gospel sanctioned as lawful among Christians, and what it prohibited as unlawful; so that the churches thus instructed might exhibit to men of all orders of mind, and to governments of every form, the practical requirements of that *New King*, whose kingdom they were engaged in setting up. That kingdom the prophets had declared was to be universal and eternal. The very first utterances of the Gospel, therefore, concerning the *extent and duration* of this kingdom, must excite solicitude among rulers and people in every nation where the Gospel was proclaimed. They must necessarily feel solicitous to know its bearings upon their respective forms of government, and their social institutions. This we know from the New Testament was the fact. And especially would they desire to know, whether its object was to break up the whole framework of society and reconstruct it on a new basis. The people and their rulers must expect that a *King*, with ambassadors and agents in every country, *to organize a universal kingdom*, could only accomplish *that object* by overthrowing the existing relations of society, and the organized governments for their security and protection. This new kingdom, they would naturally suppose, might be based on the principle of making all things common, or it might be based upon the principle of private property and personal rights. If on the principle that all things are common, then private property, matrimony, slavery, family and State governments were to be overthrown, and the antediluvian model, *in the excesses of its final licentiousness*, re-established upon their ruins.

If upon the principle of private property and personal rights, still the question would come up whether the settlement of these rights, and the relations out of which they grow, were to be left "to the powers that be," or to this *new king of universal dominion*.* To answer these questions is one great object of the apostolic letters. The passages in these letters, which sanction human governments as ordinances of God, that are to be obeyed by the disciples of Christ, have been already referred to and quoted at length.

I will now bring to the notice of my reader those portions of these letters which recognize as lawful the most important relations of society which had been established in the Roman empire, under which the Saviour and the apostles lived, and within the limits of which his kingdom was first to be set up. Husband and wife, parent and child, master and servant, ruler and people, were all relations existing in that empire, and they are all recognized by the apostles as lawful relations in the sight of God. The relative duties which grow out of the first three of these relations are enjoined in Paul's letter to the church at Ephesus, beginning at the twenty-first verse of the fifth chapter, and ending with the ninth verse of the sixth chapter, which reads thus: "Wives, submit yourselves unto your own husbands as unto the Lord. For the husband is the head of the wife, even as Christ is the head of the Church; and he is the Saviour of the body. Therefore as the Church is subject unto Christ, so *let* the wives *be* to their own husbands in every thing. Husbands, love your wives, even as Christ also loved the Church, and gave himself for it, that he might sanctify and cleanse it with the washing of water by the word; that he might present it to himself, a glorious Church, not having spot or wrinkle, or any such thing; but that it should be holy and without blemish. So ought men to love their wives as their own bodies; he that loveth his wife loveth himself. For no man ever yet hated his own flesh, but nourisheth and cherisheth it, even as the Lord, the Church; for we are members of his body, of his flesh, and of his bones. For this cause shall a man leave his father and mother, and shall be joined unto his wife, and they two shall be one flesh. This is a great mystery, but I speak concerning Christ and the Church. Nevertheless, let every one of you in particular, so love his wife even as himself, and the wife see that she reverence her husband."

"Children, obey your parents in the Lord, for this is right. Honor thy father and mother, (which is the first commandment with promise,) that it may be well with thee, and thou mayest live long on the earth. And ye fathers, provoke not your children to wrath; but bring them up in the nurture and admonition of the Lord."

"Servants, be obedient to them that are your masters according to the flesh, with fear and trembling, in singleness of your heart, as unto Christ. Not with eye-service, as men pleasers; but as the servants of Christ, doing the will of God from the heart; with good will, doing service as to the Lord, and not to men; knowing that whatsoever good thing any man doeth, the same shall he receive of the Lord, whether he be bond or free. And ye masters, do the same things unto them, forbearing threatening, knowing that your master also is in heaven; neither is there respect of persons with him."

Here is instruction for a Christian family, a domestic empire, containing within itself the elements of a state for whose welfare a system of control and subordination was established by the Roman law and sanctioned by the Saviour, in which husbands, parents and masters are invested with authority over wives, children, and slaves; and the exercise of this authority, and the yielding of this subjection cheerfully, are made to be Christian duties. Christ recognizes these relations as lawful; and he recognizes the authority and subjection which belong to them as just and right in the sight of God. He gives instruction how God is to be glorified by the parties. The husband is to glorify him by such an exercise of his authority over his wife as will prove that he loves her as himself, by a love which in character resembles that of Christ to the Church. The wife is to glorify God by a submission to her husband, which in character resembles that which is due to the Saviour by the Church. The child is to glorify God by an obedience to his parents, which God makes in his word to be right, and promises to reward with good days and long life. The father is to glorify God by such an exercise of his authority as will not provoke, and by its severity beget wrath in his child; but by such an exercise of it as will bring him up to social, moral, and intellectual manhood in the fear of God. The servant is to glorify God by an obedience to his master, the same in character as the obedience he is commanded to render to Christ. The master is to glorify God by an exercise of his authority over his servant, the same in character as the obedience required of his servant to him; that is, that he is to exercise this authority with singleness of heart as to Christ, Christ having required it to be done, and made it to be a medium of serving him, when done by a right rule and to a right end. These several reciprocal duties grow out of these several relations. Each of these relations of husband and wife, parent and child, master and servant, has the sanction and approval of God, both among the patriarchs under the law of Moses, and now by the authority of Christ, in the organic laws of his kingdom, which visibly is a gospel Church where all its ordinances are administered, its doctrines taught, and laws enforced. This being so, then I ask, if a man honors his understanding by limiting the slave's obligation, as the abolitionists do, to such duties as the slave owes to every other man as much as to his master—that is, that the slave is only bound to speak the truth, to be honest, to perform moral requirements, which are due by him to all other men as much as to his master; and that these moral requirements are *equally the duty of all men*, and do not grow out of the relation he stands in to his master.

Some of the greatest and best men in the abolition ranks have put forth such an interpretation as the above of those plain portions of God's word, and thousands, if not millions, have swallowed the poison; but these distinguished abolitionists, from *some cause*, have omitted to mention the "*obedience*" and "*subjection*" which grow out of the relation itself, and which God has *positively commanded*. Servants are positively commanded in the letter above quoted, "to obey them who are their masters according to the flesh, with fear and trembling, in singleness of their heart as unto Christ, with good will doing them service." Query.—Do the slaves of the New Testament stand in a relation to *all other men* that makes it their duty to *obey all other men* after this model? And have all men authority from God to control, direct, and receive such service as this is, from *all other men?* Again, the wife is bound to obey her husband in every thing. Now, if this obedience of the wife does not grow out of her relation to her husband, then she is bound, according to abolitionism, to *obey every other man in every thing*, and every other man has an equal right, with her husband, to *require it of her*. The slave is bound to obey his master, and to please him well. If this obligation does not grow out of the relation the slave stands in to his master, then the slave, the wife, the child, and the citizen, are all released from all the obligations of obedience in these several relations, and may inaugurate the antediluvian lawlessness and licentiousness, as more in accordance with the freedom and equality of the "higher law" of the present day.

The letter from which I have quoted was written to a church that, on two accounts, was second to no other in importance. First, for the facility with which statesmen, both in Europe and Asia, could obtain knowledge concerning the effects of Christianity on civil government; and secondly, for the influence which would be exerted by her members in this great social and commercial centre, upon men of business and pleasure who visited that city, as well as upon the members of other churches on the two adjacent continents.

In addition to the importance of Ephesus as a social, commercial, and religious centre, the apostle attached additional importance to it, from his personal knowledge of the habits of the place, and the character of the materials of which the Church was composed. He had labored here in person, night and day, for three years, going from house to house, teaching the doctrines of the Gospel, and exhorting to the discharge of its practical requirements. During this time he had invaded and overthrown, in that city, a branch of the most dangerous organization to truth which had ever existed. Satan, in every age, has succeeded among its members in securing accredited mediums of communication with the spirit world. The witch of Endor was enabled by Satan to induce sensible men to give up God's word, and resort to these mediums for knowledge, both for the present and the future world. They had an existence among Ham's descendants in Palestine. God, in his law, ordered them and idolaters to be put to death. Both were put to death for the same reason. Both exalted lying spirits above the Eternal I AM. Hence the New Testament caution, "Try the spirits." God's word under the Mosaic and Christian dispensation furnishes the test: if they speak not in agreement with that, they are not of God.

We have lately been informed of their organized existence in China, and that this organization dates back centuries before the letter of Paul to the Ephesians was written. The masters of this diabolical art, and their Satanic mediums, are among us. The mediums are perhaps as unconscious of Satanic possession, as was the damsel who followed Paul, until he turned and cast the devil out of her.

Christ was constantly ejecting Satan from the bodies of men when here on earth, and restoring them to their right minds again. The apostles were commissioned by Christ to cast out devils. These devils might, and probably did, by the agency of these masters of the diabolic art, possess men's bodies, and distract their minds. The masters of this art, whose object was gain, were persons of policy and skill. We may well suppose they were slow to venture a direct encounter with truth; but at Ephesus Paul invaded their ranks by the Gospel, and was made mighty through God in overthrowing their superstructure. He destroyed the foundation upon which it rested. That foundation was a preference in their hearts, for the master who paid the pocket, rather than the master who emptied it of cash, and then of worldly glory. The first was the devil, the other was the Saviour.

This diabolical art was propagated by a course of secret training, in which secreted books were used for subjecting the human organism to the control of lying spirits, so as to make a human being see and hear mentally, and speak audibly, as moved by another intelligent mind. Ahab's prophets were thus acted upon, we know, because God permitted Micaias to have an inspired sight of a lying spirit going forth and deceiving them. This deception was effected by giving them a false view of the future. The converts from spiritualism at Ephesus, as soon as born again by the Spirit of God, searched for these diabolical books, and gathered up and publicly burned a number of them, the price of which was fifty thousand pieces of silver; "so mightily grew the word of God and prevailed."

A distinguished man, named Demetrius, and a number of craftsmen with him, were banded together also in Ephesus, for the encouragement of idolatry, by making silver decorations for idolatrous worshippers. These craftsmen were invaded, and their craft endangered by the apostle's labors. Idolatry was as fatal to salvation by Christ, as the doctrine taught by Satanic mediums. These mediums, it is said, have now opened the seventh heaven among us. This heaven lies beyond six others, inferior to it. They shut up the Heaven of the Bible, and open others better suited to ungodly men. Idolatry, then and now, does the same thing. These idolatrous craftsmen and Satanic Spiritualists at Ephesus were either overthrown, or shorn by Paul's labors of the encouragement which kept their crafts alive. By these displays of Gospel power, nearly the whole people of Asia had their attention aroused, and were brought as a consequence to hear the Gospel.

For the progressive results of the Gospel upon a theatre so long and so extensively controlled by the highest order of Satanic agents, the apostle must have felt intense solicitude, and hence his first letter to this church, which is principally occupied upon the great doctrines of the Gospel. From this letter, a quotation has been made on the domestic relations. The apostle was moved by the Holy Ghost to give them written inspired authority for the legality of matrimony, and for the legality of slavery in the sight of God, both of which are now questioned, or condemned, by the feedom and equality doctrine of the higher law; as one, if not both, was at Ephesus. And he gave them written and inspired authority for the duties imposed upon these parties; and the duties imposed also by the Gospel upon parents and children. Thus, a door was opened, which made it proper to teach them that obedience to the commanded duties of these several relations, was a religious service; that it reflected God's glory to others, secured assurance of their own acceptance with God, and constituted visible and credible evidence that he who said he loved Christ, and did not keep these commandments, "was a liar, and the truth was not in him."

The apostle had been admonished by the Holy Spirit before he left Ephesus, that after his departure grievous wolves would come in among them, not sparing the flock, and that from among themselves, also, men would arise, "speaking perverse things, to draw away disciples after them."

In about one year from the time he wrote the letter to this church, from which I have quoted, he wrote another letter to Timothy, who was ministering to this church at the time. In this letter to Timothy, the apostle lets us know, that notwithstanding his plain instruction to this church in person for three years, and then in his letter to this church four years afterwards on the subject of slavery, men with abolition sentiments had risen up among them, who ignored his doctrine, and taught that Christianity abolished slavery, that slavery violated the unalienable right of every man to freedom and equality. Now, while these are not the identical words used by the apostle, yet this is an unavoidable inference from the language which he does use, as you will see in 1 Tim. vi. 1 to 6.

"1. Let as many servants as are under the yoke count their own masters worthy of all honor, that the name of God and his doctrine be not blasphemed.

2. And they that have believing masters, let them not despise them because they are brethren; but rather do them service, because they are faithful and beloved, partakers of the benefit. These things teach and exhort.

3. If any man teach otherwise, and consent not to wholesome words, even the words of our Lord Jesus Christ, and the doctrine which is according to godliness,

4. He is proud, knowing nothing; but doting about questions and strifes of words, whereof cometh envy, strife, railings, evil surmisings,

5. Perverse disputing of men of corrupt minds, and destitute of the truth, supposing that gain is godliness; from such withdraw thyself."

I have said above, that the language used by the apostle in the five verses I have quoted, furnishes an unavoidable inference that abolition doctrine had gotten into the church at Ephesus, and was producing the same results which it is producing now among us. In the first verse above, the apostle enjoins all servants under the yoke of bondage, to account their own masters worthy of all honor. This duty of counting masters worthy of all honor, was enjoined upon Christian slaves, who had unbelieving masters, as the next verse shows. This injunction, of all honor to unbelieving masters, constitutes a new item in the catalogue of directions to servants. It shows plainly, that a system of false teaching had made this injunction necessary. This is the first and only time we ever hear in the New Testament, of the conduct of believing slaves causing the name of God and his doctrine to be blasphemed. Blaspheming his name and doctrine is represented as a consequence originating in the insubordinate tendency of the doctrine which these believing servants had received. Now let it be noted by the reader, that the apostle had never delivered any doctrine to servants, that had an insubordinate tendency. But on the contrary, in his letter to this church one year before, he had taught servants to "obey them that were their masters according to the flesh, in singleness of heart as unto Christ, with good will doing service as unto the Lord." In the same letter, he taught the servants in that church that Christ would reward them for that service. In the second verse he teaches believing slaves, who had believing masters, that they were not to despise their masters because they were believers; but the rather to do them service, because they were faithful and beloved brethren, who would be benefited by their service. Now, why were such direction and doctrine as this necessary? Neither Paul, nor any other apostle had ever taught the servants of that, or any other church, that the doctrine of the Gospel authorized believing slaves to despise Christian masters because they were believers in Christ. Where did this anti-Christian hatred in the heart of these servants come from? Certainly, not from the teaching of the apostle. He taught obedience to masters with good will from the heart, whether they were believing or unbelieving masters. He taught that God required this of them, and that when they rendered it, they were to render it as to God; which made it a part of their religious service. The doctrine which begat hatred in their hearts to their masters, was a doctrine taught by some one else, who did not consent to the wholesome words of our Lord Jesus Chrst on this subject (referred to by the apostle in the 3d verse). This being the state of facts, the apostle tells Timothy in the second verse that he was to teach servants "to honor their masters, and to serve them with good will from the heart, as to the Lord"—to teach, that this was their duty, made so by the Saviour,—that he must "teach and exhort" them to the discharge of this duty, that God might be glorified, his doctrine honored, and scandal avoided. He then tells Timothy, that "if any man teach otherwise, and consent not to the wholesome words of Christ"—and would not wipe his hands of all responsibility for such treasonable and insubordinate sentiments in the Church, it would be proof that he was "proud, knowing nothing" on this subject, that he was in rebellion against Christ; and therefore he orders Timothy at the end of the fifth verse, that from all such character she must "withdraw himself." In the fourth and fifth verses, he tells Timothy the description of characters such abolition sentiments produce, and how such characters employed themselves. Now if such characters were not already in Ephesus, then why does the apostle speak of their character and conduct?—and why command to withdraw from them?

We can and we ought to compare the abolitionists of the present day with the abolitionism at Ephesus, or with the description given of it by the apostle. If they are identically the same, then we run no risk in assigning to each the same father.

The apostle says of the abolitionist at Ephesus, "he is proud, knowing nothing"—that is, he knows nothing of God's will concerning slavery, as that will has been announced by his Spirit in the Bible; or if he knows it to be in the Bible, then he does not submit to the Bible as authority.

These five verses bring to our notice the doctrine of Divine subordination established under the Gospel between masters and servants. They bring to our notice also, by unavoidable inference, the teachers of a doctrine that is subversive of this subordination both in Church and State. The moral character and conduct ascribed to those who subvert the doctrine of Divine subordination, in Church and State, is also brought to view in the small compass of these five verses, and at the end of them, a command is given to withdraw from the opposers of Divine subordination.

The question comes up: Who are they from whom, by this command, Christians are required to withdraw themselves? Can individuals be ascertained from their character and with as much certainty, as that light and darkness are not the same? I think so, for the following reasons: First, there are classes of individuals at the present day, who teach what the apostle forbade to be taught; that is, that servants under the yoke of bondage are not bound by the law of God to count their masters worthy of all honor; who teach that all laws which subject men to slavery are laws which disgrace the civilization of the world. Secondly, there are classes of individuals who teach that such laws ought not to be obeyed, and that resistance to them is the highest style of Christian duty. Thirdly, there are large classes who teach that slavery is the greatest of sins; the sum of all villainy. There are classes who teach that the slave, so far from honoring his master with all honor, ought to run away from his master, to steal his property, to burn his house, and in every way to resist these New Testament directions. Organized abolition is a unit, made up of thousands, if not of millions, of individuals, who are actively and zealously engaged in teaching all the abolition opposition to the laws of God and men, that I have specified above, and much more of the same kind. They are banded together, not only to teach it, but to carry out their teaching, by overthrowing slavery and the sovereignty of the slave States, at whatever cost of life and suffering, so that four millions of happy slaves shall be made free from labor, to perish of want.

Now, my reader, I must be permitted to say that the abolitionists of this country and Europe are engaged in teaching a doctrine which is plainly and palpably at war with a most important doctrine of the New Testament—that of civil and ecclesiastical subordination. A doctrine so dangerous to the peace, prosperity, and happiness of the Church and State, makes it the imperative duty of all Christians to withdraw from all ecclesiastical connection with them. This the apostle expressly charges Timothy to do. No Christian man who knows what abolitionism teaches, and who wishes honestly and sincerely to know from whom the apostle requires him to withdraw himself, can be at a loss in deciding that abolitionists are the characters. They teach "otherwise," and expressly contrary on the subject of slavery, to the teaching of the apostle in this place, and in every other part of the New Testament on the same subject. And not only contrary to the *New Testament*, but to the teaching of the Almighty to the patriarchs, and in the law of Moses on the same subject. This I have previously made so apparent by the quotations and references from the Old Testament, as to leave every man, I think, who reads it, without excuse for saying or believing that the Bible condemns slavery.

The dangerous tendency of this political and ecclesiastical heresy, called abolitionism, is exhibited by the apostle, when in the third, fourth, and fifth verses above quoted, he sets forth the moral elements it calls into activity in the human heart, after men are brought under its dominion. He says, such persons are "proud." Pride is inordinate self-esteem, a high conceit of one's own excellence. "Knowing nothing," of course he means, as to the will of God on slavery. Now, this part of the inspired description of abolitionism shows up to human view from the Bible, a zealous body of men engaged in constructing society on a new basis. For its fundamental principle, they claim the sanction of God's word. The inspired apostle affirms in so many words, they are ignorant of God's will on the subject. That, of that will they "know nothing." That the Divine principle of subordination, which they seek to overthrow, lies at the bottom of all society which has God's sanction. This is the principle they are laboring to overthrow, in order that they may substitute the freedom and equality principle in the place of it,—a principle which is unknown in any divinely organized body, domestic, political, ecclesiastical, or animal. Insubordination is taught to servants, and if to them, then for the same reason it must be extended to all the other relations among men, which subject one to the control of another.

These characters at Ephesus are further noticed by the apostle in the fourth verse, as to the plan they pursued to accomplish their object. The apostle describes them as "doting about questions." "Doting" is defined to be excessive fondness. It means, therefore, an excessive fondness for questions. A moderate acquaintance with abolitionists, will suggest that this fondness for questions is a peculiarity with them, a distinguished trait of character. Their questions are numberless, they are stereotyped, and so shaped as to imply a great deal not expressed, as taking for granted a great deal neither admitted nor susceptible of proof, as to suggest false issues, and parry off legitimate premises. These questions, for which this doting fondness is made prominent by the inspired pen, are questions which form the intellectual atmosphere, out of which the abolitionist cannot breathe. Subject him to the atmosphere of God's word on this subject, and he dies,—at least such has been the result, as far as I have seen it tried.

One remark will unravel the whole stock of abolition legerdemain involved in these questions. The design of these questions is, to make the lawfulness of slavery look too monstrous in the sight of God, for human belief. Their plan to accomplish this, is to parade its greatest abuses, and its worst laws. If facts are wanting as to these, then they are manufactured to order. Well, my reader, admitting all the facts of abuse which have ever existed, or been charged to exist, and all the bad laws said to be found on the statute books, to be veritable facts, and then admitting that the half has never been told or imagined; what does it prove in settling this question:—"*Is slavery a lawful relation in the sight of God?*"—the Bible being judge. Will all these facts of abuse go further in proving slavery to be an unlawful relation among men, than the same description of facts will go to prove that husband and wife—parent and child—ruler and people, are unlawful relations in the sight of God? It certainly will not; because such abuses are found in all these relations. An honest and candid man will be obliged to admit, that if the abuses of authority and subordination, in *any one* of these relations, will prove that relation to be unlawful, unjust, and sinful; then for the same reason, they are all proved to be unlawful, unjust, and sinful. For the admission of this, no sane man is prepared.

The word of God expressly sanctions all of these relations, prescribes the duties which belong to all of them—and forbids all the abuses and wrongs which grow out of them.

The question is not—Can God sanction government when rulers oppress their subjects?—Can God sanction marriage, when husbands do not love their wives as themselves, but abuse their authority over them? The question is not—Can God sanction the government of fathers over their children, when fathers abuse their authority?—Can God sanction slavery when masters abuse their authority over their slaves? But the question to be settled is this:—Does the word of God establish and sanction these several relations, enjoin the duties growing out of them, and make disobedience to the law of duty to be sin, just as he does disobedience to any other commanded duty?

All the questions, which a doting fondness for questions can induce an abolitionist to ask, will never change the issue. That issue is to be decided by the Bible. It is to be decided by a yea, or a nay, to this question: Does the Bible sanction the relation of master and slave; prescribing their relative duties, and making obedience to those duties, obligatory on Christians, as a service rendered to Christ?

To return from this digression, I will proceed in noticing the moral elements which this ecclesiastical and political heresy calls into activity, according to the description given of them by the inspired pen, eighteen hundred years ago. The next item in the catalogue is "strifes of words." Strifes of words is defined to be, exertion, or contention for superiority in intellectual efforts, as to what words mean. This strife about the meaning of words has been carried on by the abolitionists, until the best intellects among them are not ashamed to ignore the import of words which have had a universally accepted meaning among the ripest scholars of the world since Moses wrote the law, and the apostles wrote the New Testament. Their strifes about words have perverted or denied the meaning of words, and thereby created false mediums, through which an abolitionist sees in his mind what has no existence in the words used. This is as fatal to truth as spiritual mediums.

The next item of the moral elements of abolitionism enumerated by the apostle, is "envy." Envy is defined "discontent, excited by the sight of another's superiority, accompanied with hatred"—"a hatred springing from mortified pride and ambition that another has obtained what one has a strong desire to possess." The next moral element in the apostle's catalogue of abolitionism is, "strife." Strife is defined to be, exertion, or contention for superiority"—"either by physical, or intellectual efforts." The next element enumerated is, "railings." Railings is defined to be, "clamoring with insulting language, uttering reproachful words." The next characteristic in this moral picture is, "evil surmising." Surmising is defined to be, "suspecting, imagining upon slight evidence." The next characteristic is, "perverse disputings." Perverse, is an adjective used to denote the quality of a thing. The thing here is, "disputings." The character of the disputant is set forth in the word "perverse." Perverse is defined to be, "obstinate in the wrong, disposed to be contrary, untractable." These perverse disputants are described by the apostle, as men "of corrupt minds." Corrupt is defined to be, "change from a sound to a putrid state"—"a change from good to bad." In the next item the subjects of abolitionism are represented by the apostle, as men "destitute of the truth." This part of his description, *condemns them as teachers*, and is a warning against them as dangerous leaders. No man, "destitute of the truth," can be fit to lead others. In concluding the character of the abolitionists at Ephesus, the apostle identifies them in character with Simon the sorcerer, who supposed, with these abolitionists, that "gain was godliness"—that is to say, if godliness did not break up all subordination between the inferior and superior man, and give freedom and equality to the subordinated man, then it was not worthy to be called godliness, because it could not have God for its author, inasmuch as God, in their opinion, "created all men free and equal."

Here is an analysis of the moral qualities of abolitionism, as given to the world by an inspired pen. Can any man truthfully say, that its characteristics, at the present time, are not *faithfully and truly set forth* in the drawing made of it at Ephesus, eighteen hundred years ago?

Now, my reader, I have quoted the recognition of slavery by the Apostle Paul in his letter to the Ephesian church, and in his letter to Timothy, while Timothy was ministering to that church one year afterwards. The slavery of which he writes was Roman slavery. The slaves he addressed were the property of masters. The masters' power over them, was unlimited by the Roman law. The masters and slaves were members of the Church of Christ. Now the question naturally arises, Did God command these believing masters to free their slaves? Did he teach them that slavery was the greatest sin among men? Did he teach them that every man was created free and equal? Did he teach them that every man had an unalienable right to life, liberty, and the pursuit of happiness? And did God teach these believing slaves, that they had as much right to freedom as their masters? Did he teach them they had as much right to enslave their masters, as their masters had to hold them in slavery? Did God teach these slaves, that it was *not their duty* to obey their masters, but that it *was their duty to assert and maintain their freedom* by the use of all means in their power? This is the doctrine of the abolitionists of the present day; but it is the very doctrine the apostle declares to be an ungodly doctrine, a doctrine not according to godliness, a blasphemous doctrine; and he commands Christians to withdraw from all such as hold or teach it. And the reason why they should withdraw he gives to be this,—"that the name of God and his doctrine" of civil subordination "be not blasphemed."

We will now hear the Apostle Paul instructing Titus, whom he left in Crete, to guard the Church against false doctrine. In the 2d. chapter, 9th and 10th verses, he says: "Exhort servants to be obedient unto their own masters, and to please them well in all things; not answering again; not purloining,; but showing all good fidelity, that they may adorn the doctrine of God our Saviour in all things." Here my reader will see that he makes it the duty of Titus to exhort Roman slaves, who were believers, to be obedient to their own masters, and to please them well in all things. Now, I ask, is this the teaching and exhortation of abolitionists? He charges Titus to teach them not to purloin. Purloining is defined to be, "to take, or carry away for one's self." Is this the teaching of abolitionists? No, it is exactly the contrary of their teaching. He instructs Titus to teach them "to show all good fidelity to their masters." Fidelity is defined to be, "faithfulness—a careful and exact observance of duty, or performance of obligations." Is this the teaching of abolitionists? And why is this required by the apostle of the servant? The next words tell us why. It is that they "may adorn the doctrine of God our Saviour in all things." This obedience and fidelity of the servant, then, are to make the doctrine of God our Saviour on slavery appear beautiful—"to decorate it." This is defined to be the meaning of "adorn." *Question.*—Is this the doctrine taught by the abolitionists? Do they teach that the service, obedience, and fidelity of slaves to their masters, rendered with good will from the heart, decorate and beautify the doctrine taught by God our Saviour? No, my reader; but the insubordinate doctrine they do teach, is declared by the apostle to be blasphemy against the doctrine of godliness taught by God our Saviour, as you will see in so many words in 1 Tim. vi. 1.

I will now present my reader with Paul's teaching to the Colossian church, on the subject of slavery. This church he had never seen, but hearing they had been called by the Gospel into a church state, he wrote them a letter. The great doctrine of salvation by Christ, is his theme in the commencement of this letter. After unfolding Christ's divinity, the sufficiency of his sacrifice for the atonement of sin, of his righteousness for the justification of the ungodly and their completeness when united to him, he proceeds to show them how they are to glorify God, by a course of conduct prescribed by God their Saviour. "That they were to forbear one another, to forgive one another, to put on charity, to let the peace of God rule in their hearts, to be thankful, to let the word of God dwell in them richly, to do every thing in the name of the Lord Jesus; that wives submit themselves to their own husbands, that husbands love their wives, that children obey their parents, that fathers provoke not their children;" and then in chap. iii. 22, "that servants obey in all things their masters, according to the flesh; not with eye service as men pleasers, but in singleness of heart, fearing God: and whatsoever ye do, do it heartily as to the Lord, and not unto men, knowing that of the Lord ye shall receive the reward of the inheritance; for ye serve the Lord Christ. But he that doeth wrong, shall receive for the wrong which he hath done, and there is no respect of persons. Masters, give unto your servants that which is just and equal; knowing that ye also have a master in heaven." To understand any special instruction, it is necessary to understand the condition and circumstances of those to whom the instruction is given. This instruction was given to Roman servants and masters, who were converted to Christianity. These servants were their masters' money or property. By the Roman law they were bound to service or labor for life. They were bought and sold as any other species of property. In these respects their condition resembled American slaves. Their Roman masters, although converted to Christianity, had power by the Roman law to coerce obedience by any means they might think proper to use, and were responsible to that law for no cruelty they might practise. In this there is no resemblance between Roman and American slavery. The American slave is protected by law, and secured in comfort. His service or labor is secured to the master. For this service or labor the master is legally bound for more than justice could demand as an equivalent—and that paid in the best form.

Notwithstanding all this, our Northern brethren have allowed themselves to believe that Southern slavery is as bad as Roman slavery. No wonder, therefore, that it should awaken their sympathy. Now let us suppose, for argument's sake, that Southern slavery is as bad as Roman slavery was; what would our abolition brethren gain by the admission? Can they induce the world to believe that they have reached a perfection that renders them more susceptible of sympathy than the Saviour? They know that the Saviour had Roman slavery before his eyes constantly to awaken his sympathy, and they believe he had the power to abolish it at any time, as much as he had to control the winds and waves of Galilee. Would it not then be respectful to him to inquire how this almighty power of his was exercised for securing the gratification of his sympathetic heart, and how his infinite benevolence manifested itself for the down-trodden and helpless slave of the Roman empire? To the man who will not consent to do this, we may safely apply the description given of an Ephesian abolitionist in vi. Tim.; that is, "that he is proud." Pride is an unreasonable conceit of one's own superiority, but is there a man on earth, who thinks himself the superior of Christ in benevolence and sympathy? Of that I will leave my reader to judge, by the evidence which he may possess for the settlement of such a question. This much is certain, however, that Jesus Christ had slavery before his eyes every day, and knew that it existed everywhere in a worse form than any that now exists in Asia, Europe, or America.

I have made the above quotation from Paul's letter to the Colossians, that my reader might see how Christ's sympathy showed itself towards the slave, and how his authority was put forth upon the master. This pattern of sympathy was given by infinite wisdom and benevolence. It certainly ought to be followed by us. This pattern enjoins obedience upon the slave to his master, in all things; and this obedience secures to the master the service and labor of the slave—but it does not stop there. It demands of the slave, not only this service to the letter, but it demands a moral character for this service. With that character, Christ promises to accept this service from the slave as a service done to him; and assures the slave that when this literal service to his earthly master is rendered, with the moral qualities in his heart towards that master which Christ requires of him, that then this service will be worthy of that reward which his heavenly master has promised to them that obey him.

On the other hand, a moral character is required for the master's authority, exercised over his servant, which in justice and equity shall resemble that of his heavenly master. This is the way Jesus Christ expressed his sympathy for the poor down-trodden slave of the Roman empire. He did not abolish the relation that the slave stood in to his master. He did not teach him to rebel, to run away, to murder, or steal. He never hinted to the slave the "freedom and equality" doctrine. But by a single breath from his righteous lips to the master, secured a greater moral reform to the world, than all the emancipations that have taken place from that time until this. There is truly moral power put forth for good, in the obedience enjoined upon the slave, and especially in the duty to the slave, enjoined upon the master.

Question.—Was Christ as capable of feeling sympathy as men of the present day? Was he as capable as men of the present day of expressing his sympathy in the best form?

Question.—Is all that he felt, and all that he did, in reference to slavery, infinitely right, and infinitely perfect? If he was "God manifested in the flesh," this *must be so.* And if this be so, then there is, in our country, the most daring and high-handed rebellion against God, on this subject, that has ever been practised since he said, "ye are my friends, if ye do whatsoever I say unto you." The principle of subordination, sought to be overthrown, is vital in Church and State. The infidel principle of "freedom and equality," sought to be established on its ruins, is unknown to the Bible, contradicted by all experience, and subversive of all government among men.

The next inspired instruction I will present to my reader on the subject of slavery, is in Paul's letter to the Corinthian church. Nothing was more familiar at that time to the minds of men than slavery in Corinth, and all the adjacent sections of the European and Asiatic continents. On the subject of slavery the apostle, in his letter to the church, lays down a general principle to guide Christians in this and other relations they may sustain to society, while the world stands. It is this, "that every man abide in the same calling wherein he was called." In chap. vii. 1 to 25, you will find his meaning to be this: that if a man was called being a servant, the Gospel did not free him; if free, the Gospel did not enslave him; if married, the Gospel did not divorce him; if single, the Gospel did not compel him to marry. These were all relations among men that were sanctioned of God. The Gospel corrected their abuses, by prescribing their duties. The omission of these duties was made to be sin against God. The context shows that the apostle advised slaves and all others to remain as they were called. "Art thou called being a servant? care not for it;" and advises, "if thou mayest be free, use it rather," which was understood, until Calvin's day, to mean, use slavery rather. I have no doubt from the context in the 20th and 24th verses, and the circumstances of the times, that Paul would advise a preference for slavery over freedom, to the slaves of this church, and to all other slaves with Christian masters, placed in circumstances analogous to those which then existed. If his advice to unmarried persons, in the 8th and 9th verses, and in the 26th and 27th, to remain single during that time of trouble, was good advice, then for the same reason his advice to Christian slaves with Christian masters, not to accept freedom if offered to them, was good advice also. In slavery to Christian masters, they were provided with homes, could remain with their families, were provided with food and raiment, were free from anxious worldly care, and could wait upon the Lord without distraction. If freed, they would have nothing to depend on for the support of themselves and their families, but their daily labor, and, in addition, would have the burdens of government to meet, and the perils of war to encounter. In assuming the responsibilities of freedom, they would have many competitors for the rewards of labor and merit. These competitors, for the time being, would be better qualified than themselves to obtain the prize. With such facts before the apostle's mind, and with his experience of actual life, he could scarcely fail to advise Christian slaves, who were without experience and proper qualifications for the successful use of freedom, to use bondage rather, if freedom should be offered them by a Christian master. This would be the advice, it seems to me, of any sensible, good man, to a slave under like circumstances. From the context, I take this without doubt to be the apostle's advice. In any event, however, as to what he meant by, "use it rather," the doctrine as to the lawfulness of slavery is the same.

Now let us glance at the antagonism between the teaching of God to this church on the subject of slavery, and the teaching of abolitionism. God teaches a slaveholding church to let every man abide in the same calling wherein he was called; that is, "if thou art called being a servant, care not for it"—that slavery is a condition that should not awaken a care in his mind. Care not for it, says God to the slave. Abolitionism teaches that he should care so much for it, as to assert his liberty, and, if necessary to secure it, he may murder his master, steal his property, burn his house, escape from his service, and use every means to overthrow his master, and the government under which his master lives, if it takes peace from the earth, and all the blessings of civilization.

Can any two things be more opposite than this teaching? No wonder the apostle should charge Christians to withdraw from all who teach a doctrine that must, when carried to its legitimate results, overthrow all subordination among men, and involve the world in anarchy and blood.

I feel almost ashamed, that in a Christian country any man should be called upon to prove slavery to be a relation which God, in his word, sanctions as lawful. Every man, from the time he begins to know any thing, begins to know that the principle of slavery, and that slavery itself, to some extent, is an indispensable element in every form of government. The extent of the control is to be measured by the capacity of the subject on which it acts. This is the prominent principle in every vitalized organization of the material world, as well as those organizations ordained and sanctioned of God for social purposes.

The subordination of the inferior to the superior stands prominently to view in every thing that comes from the hand of infinite wisdom. Rebellion against this principle peopled the realms of darkness with those who were once the angels of light. The same thing brought upon us "all our woe." The Gospel of the Son of God was designed to re-establish the dominion of this principle. When this object is accomplished, the wilderness and the solitary place of the human heart are seen to bud and blossom as the rose. The rebellion of abolitionism against this principle, as an element in the social structure, is active, and dangerous in the highest degree to regulated liberty and Christian civilization. If the Bible was duly reverenced, and but slightly examined, the evil could be corrected. But when we see men who are eminently intellectual, professing allegiance to Christ, and claiming, at the same time, his authority for doing and teaching what he has in his word denominated blasphemy, it awakens unavoidably the painful foreboding which the inspiring Spirit authorizes in this declaration: "Because they receive not the love of the truth, that they might be saved," "God, for this cause, shall send them strong delusion, that they should believe a lie, that they all might be damned who believe not the truth, but have pleasure in unrighteousness." The truth of God on slavery is not believed, and unrighteousness, of the most crimson hue, has given among us the highest pleasure to abolitionists. They are seeking to overthrow governments whose models have the express sanction of the Almighty. The Scriptures I have quoted from the Old Testament, prove that God ordained at Mount Sinai a slave government for his own people; and those quoted from the New Testament prove that Christ, by the apostles, sanctioned slave governments organized by men, as ordinances of God.

It would be quite as creditable to claim the character of benefactors and philanthropists for crusaders in favor of freedom and equality among the members of the human body, as among the members of the social body. Let each member of our bodies be personified—then invest the foot with as much right to control and govern the eye, as the eye has to control and govern the foot, and so on of all the rest of our members, and in this you will have a fair sample of what is now going on. The foot, with the aid and control of the eye, is as useful and as necessary as any other member of the body, for securing and participating in the general and harmonious result of a subordinated set of members, which altogether make up our body. But when the control of the eye is taken away, and the foot, unaided and uncontrolled by the eye, commences its work in the thorny and dangerous path of life, upon the "freedom and equality" principle, you will soon see a result which resembles the result in a social body under the same abolition and infidel principle.

I know very well that the masses at the North have been artfully subjected by the school, the pulpit, and the press, to a system of teaching which has left them ignorant of God's word on the subject of slavery. I know there yet lives in many of their hearts a reverence for that word, which would secure for it a control over their consciences, if they knew its teachings on this subject. Hoping that God in his providence will make me an humble instrument in opening the eyes of some such, I have penned these pages. I feel that the necessity for such an effort is a scandal to a Christian people; for certain I am, that no article of the Christian faith is better sustained by the Bible, than is that of slavery.

Having quoted the Apostle of the Gentiles in his inspired letters to Gentile churches on the subject of slavery, before I close, I will quote Peter on the same subject, who was the Apostle of the Jews. He felt, in the latter years of his life, great solicitude for his scattered brethren, who were persecuted and enslaved throughout the extended region of their dispersion, along the western boundary of Asia, and the eastern boundary of Europe, from the Mediterranean to the Black Sea, and thence along the northern boundary of what is called the Lesser Asia. This had long been the theatre of their dispersion and suffering. But many of them, hearing the Gospel, had enlisted in the service of Christ. The apostle well knew their character for disloyalty to other governments, and how unwilling they were, as Jews, to be subjected to the control of Gentiles—either in a domestic or political relation. And hence the instruction he gives them concerning government as an ordinance of God; and hence the exhortation he gives them to yield submission to every ordinance of man for the Lord's sake. See chap. ii. 11 to chap. iii. 18 of 1 Peter. Here you will find that the same political and domestic relations are enumerated, as those enunciated by the Apostle Paul—the same subjection to government enjoined—and the same moral character demanded for their political obedience as that required by the Apostle Paul. You will find also that the same authority for husbands and masters is sanctioned, and the same subjection of wives and servants enjoined, as that by the Apostle of the Gentiles—and the same moral characteristics are demanded for the authority exercised by the superior, and the subordination rendered by the inferior. It is made on both sides a part of Christian duty by both of these apostles. They make it to be a service rendered to God as well as to men.

Now, to lay this instruction of the Apostle Peter, with all the circumstances belonging to it, by the side of the abolition instruction, and what do we see? On the one side we see an ambassador of Christ, enjoining upon his own flesh and blood political submission, in a Christian spirit, to governments which sanction slavery; to governments which had failed to furnish guards against the abuses of the master; to governments which were created and administered by an idolatrous people; and enjoining also obedience, with good will from the heart, on Christian slaves to idolatrous as well as Christian masters. And it is worthy of further remark, that this obedience was enjoined upon slaves who were the descendants of Shem and Japheth, who were capable of exercising freedom; and not upon Ham's race, who were devoted to slavery by the Almighty. See Gen. ix. 24 to 27, before referred to. On the other side, we see men blaspheming this doctrine of political and servile obedience taught by Peter, not because the obedience is rendered to idolatrous governments and idolatrous masters, but because it is rendered to Christian governments and to Christian masters. They are not only blaspheming the doctrine, but exerting every nerve to subject men to the belief, that such servile obedience as Peter's doctrine calls for is the greatest sin on earth; and that governments which enjoin it, ought not to be honored or obeyed, whatever reverence for God or good will for men their subjects may feel and practise. And that rebellion and treason against such government are virtues, for which the perpetrators are destined to wear the brightest honors of heaven.

Can there be harmony between things so unlike, as the teachings of Peter and the teachings of the abolitionists? Can these streams come from the same fountain? Can our abolition brethren be as safe to follow as Christ and the apostles? One teaches "freedom and equality;" the other teaches inequality and subordination One leads to anarchy, the other to order. One leads to love, the other to hatred. One leads to war, the other to peace. Either liberty or civilization, or both, must die when the world is subjected to the control of their leading principle of "freedom and equality" among men. It is self-destroying when adopted, and seeks to destroy all governments which do not recognize it.

There remains another letter to be noticed, which was written by the Apostle Paul. It is his letter to Philemon. I am often reminded by the existence and contents of this letter, of the character given by the apostle to the word of God. There is a fulness, suitableness, and perfection ascribed to the Scriptures, which, it is said, leave us in ignorance on no subject of which, as Christians, it is essential for us to have knowledge. By the Scriptures the man of God is said to be thoroughly furnished with all the knowledge necessary for guiding him in every good word and work. Little, perhaps, did the apostle think, that in writing this short letter, he was erecting a standard by which not only *men* were to measure and be measured, but a standard by which *States* were to measure and be measured, not only in *moral* and *social*, but also in *personal* and *national righteousness*. This letter is so full of Divine Magic, that moral putridity in individuals and States can be unmasked by it, as readily as by the Saviour when he exposed the rottenness to view, which lay concealed beneath beautifully whited sepulchres.

Before the writing of this letter, no Scripture furnished the information which is now needed—that is, in a form that cannot be misunderstood. In the progress of human events, this information was not needed until the nineteenth century. But the precise information which this letter furnishes is now wanting. It is wanting to show the sin which men are now committing against God and men—not only in opposing slavery, but in refusing to deliver up fugitive slaves.

Among all the covenants made by nations involving the obligations of morality and good neighborship up to the eighteenth century, there was none to deliver up fugitive slaves to their owners. During Solomon's reign, Shimei pursued and recovered two of his slaves who had taken refuge with Achish, son of the king in a neighboring State. They were delivered up on application of the owner—and national comity, as in that case, has frequently been practised in regard to fugitives from labor and fugitives from justice. But no solemn covenant has ever been entered into by nations to deliver them up on application of their owners, until the original sovereign States which formed this Union covenanted to do so. When this compact was entered into, the obligation of an oath was relied on; and by the solemnities of an oath, the parties to this compact, in the person of their agents, bound themselves before heaven and earth to deliver up fugitive slaves.

Paul little thought, when writing this letter by a fugitive slave, and returning him to his Christian master, (who was also a minister of the Gospel,) and most affectionately entreating that Christian master to receive this fugitive again and to forgive him, and binding himself in writing to pay that master for all which this slave had stolen or wrongfully taken from him—that it would prove as leaven hid in three measures of meal, until it produced such a sense of what was just, and proper, and right, and Christian-like, as to induce thirteen sovereign States, seventeen hundred and twenty-nine years after that letter was written, to copy his example, and bind themselves in a solemn covenant to imitate him in their future course of national conduct. How painful it is to see the moral power of this inspired example dying away under the sway of infidelity, which repudiates the Bible, and proclaims "freedom and equality," where God in his word teaches there is none.

Here is an incident in the providence of God, so remarkably surrounded with peculiarities, as to make it on this subject a complete compendium of all that is written in the Bible on the subject of slavery.

If all other instructions given to the Church and the world were blotted out from the Bible, there would still remain in what this little letter contains, all the doctrine, and all the duty, which belong to the whole subject. And a complete and perfect answer would be furnished by it, to all the questions which can suggest themselves to an honest and candid mind, as to the will of God, and the duty of men on the subject of slavery.

The letter presents us with a runaway slave. It informs us that that slave in a distant country from his master, is converted to Christianity through the agency of the Apostle Paul. That the apostle was a prisoner at that time in the city of Rome. This convert lets the apostle know that he is a slave, and that he had fled from his master. There was no law in the Roman empire by which it was made the apostle's duty to have this slave returned to his master. There was no specific law from Christ or the Holy Spirit through the apostles, requiring the *Church*—or enjoining any of her members—to do this. This letter informs us that the master of this slave was a Christian; that he was known to the apostle to be not only a Christian, but a preacher of the Gospel; and not only a preacher, but a preacher standing high in the apostle's esteem for those qualities which adorn the private and official character of a Christian minister. The apostle, after this slave's conversion, was so delighted with his Christian deportment that he felt a deep interest in him, and cherished a most intense affection for him.

The letter informs us that the apostle was advanced in years, had long been bound with the prisoner's chain, and was daily looking for the sentence of a prejudiced tribunal that would end his life. He was poor, and occupied a position which made his friends quail under the expression of sympathy for him. In this trying condition he found his fugitive convert pre-eminently fitted to minister to him, and that he took great pleasure in doing so. Upon the master of this slave the apostle had the strongest claims for any favor he might ask of him. Any man under like circumstances, who was not the immediate representative of God, in word and deed, would have first written to the master, and begged as a favor that the slave might remain and minister to him. Any man without intense feelings of responsibility to God and men for every word he spoke, and every act he performed, would have allowed his *condition*, under such circumstances, to furnish a *sanction* for retaining this servant until the master could be heard from. How completely this case is invested with all the circumstances which can give weight and character to the lesson God designed to teach by it! The running away of this slave, his conversion to Christ by the Apostle of the Gentiles, in a distant country, its connection with the apostle's condition at the time, and with his personal acquaintance and high estimate of this slave's master, his high claims upon that master, his assigning the injustice of appropriating to his comfort what belonged to another man as the reason for sending the slave home: putting these things together, can any man on earth read this letter, and allow it to expand in his thoughts to the circumference of its plain import, and then look his fellow-man in the face and say, that slavery is a sin; that to return a fugitive slave to his master is sinful! In the light of this case no man on earth can believe it.

We of this Union have solemnly bound ourselves to deliver up fugitive slaves to their masters. The Apostle Paul was under no such covenant obligation. No earthly law bound him to do it. No New Testament statute had been delivered, which in so many words required it of him; yet he did it, because he was guided by inspiration, invested with an office, and placed in a condition that made his conduct in this whole matter *an authoritative law of Christianity*, so plainly written that all men who seek to glorify God by acting out his will, in justice and righteousness on this subject, cannot misunderstand it.

The apostle, in complying with the demands of justice to the master by sending his slave back to him again, and in exemplifying the doctrine of Christ, which requires of us whatsoever is just, whatsoever is honest, whatsoever is of good report, and especially that we act out the spirit as well as the letter, of loyalty to government as God's ordinance—deprived himself of all the soothing sympathy and suitable assistance which this converted slave could have rendered him, that he might by his conduct let the pure and unalloyed righteousness demanded by Christianity shine out like the sun, so that all men could see what the will of God was under like circumstances. He had taught this will in person to the churches. He had sent it to them, and to the evangelists, in letters. He now embodies all he had taught, and the legitimate results of his teachings, in his conduct. Our fathers entered into a covenant to carry on the righteous course of conduct exhibited by this inspired example. But, alas! their covenant is now declared to be "a covenant with hell," and a breach of it a passport to earthly honor.

OBJECTIONS ANSWERED.

There was a statute which forbade the Israelites to deliver up fugitive slaves. The abolitionists teach that this law acted on the slaves of the Israelites. This is not so. It acted not on their slaves, but on the slaves of the nations around them. It was in that day, and has been ever since, a practice among nations not to deliver up fugitives from labor or justice, unless it suited their policy and pleasure to do so. As a matter of comity it has at times been practised. When these sovereign States formed a Federal Union, they agreed by a solemn covenant to deliver up to their masters fugitive slaves who fled from another State. The Almighty forbade the Jews to do this, because the slaves who fled to them fled from idolatrous masters, and idolatrous nations around them.

These idolatrous nations and their idolatry were devoted to destruction by the Almighty. To have delivered up these fugitives, therefore, to their idolatrous and cruel masters again, would have been equivalent to putting them to death, because death awaited them on their return.

Again, by a law of the Israelites, Deut. xvii. 2 to 7, if any person practised, or was *guilty* of idolatry among them, he was immediately punished with death. The fugitive from an idolatrous nation, who fled to them, must therefore renounce his idolatry or incur the penalty of this law; he could not continue an idolater and live. Had the Israelites been permitted to deliver him up to his idolatrous master, they would have presented the strange anomaly of giving aid and encouragement to that very idolatry they were commissioned to exterminate.

The law, as I have said, had nothing to do with the slaves of the Israelites when they fled from their masters. The Almighty had given the Israelites legal authority to purchase slaves, made these slaves property, bound them to service or labor, and passed a law authorizing their masters to transmit them as an inheritance to their children forever. See Levit. xxv. 44, 45, 46. Sarah's slave-maid Hagar ran away from her mistress. The Almighty sent an angel from heaven to order her back to her mistress again. Onesimus, a slave man, ran away from his Christian master Philemon. The Apostle Paul sent this slave, when converted, back to his master again. These, I should suppose, might be taken as safe patterns to follow, under like circumstances, unless we are better than angels or apostles.

There was another statute in the Mosaic law which forbade stealing and selling of men. The abolitionists teach that this law proves slavery did not exist among the Israelites. There is such a law as this in all the slave States of the world, and it is the legal existence of slavery that renders such a law necessary. Where there is no slavery there is no need for this law. While all slave States however forbid the *stealing* of free men or slaves, they sanction and regulate by law the *buying* and *selling* of slaves, as *did* the *Mosaic law*. What the Mosaic law forbade was the *stealing* of Hebrews who were free, and making slaves of them, Deut. xxiv. 7. Or *stealing* any man to make *gain* of *him*, Exo. xxi. 16. Where the service or labor of men in any country is made property by law, then, as a matter of course, rogues are tempted to steal them, just as they are any other species of property which is valuable; and for the same reason they are tempted to steal free men and make slaves of them, and hence the *necessity for such a law.*

NOTE.—According to the Bible the Almighty subjected the Egyptians to national bondage by Joseph, and afterwards, with tokens of anger, released the Israelites by Moses from national bondage to the Egyptians. How is this apparent inconsistency to be accounted for? It is easily accounted for if we let the Scriptures be our teacher. The descendants of Ham, in Gen. ix. 25, 26, 27, are devoted to slavery, and Shem and Japheth are made their masters. In the days of Jacob, Ham's descendants in Egypt were free, and were about to perish for the want of proper qualifications to use freedom. God sent Shem, in the person of Joseph, to subject them to a more efficient government than they were capable of inaugurating or disposed to exercise. One hundred and fifty years after this the descendants of Ham, by the power of numbers and the worst of motives, subjected in the same kingdom the descendants of Shem to their control. They soon demonstrated, by imbecility and merciless cruelty, that the inferior ought not to rule over the superior race. Hence the Almighty made a most signal display of his displeasure against such unnatural subordination, and the savage cruelty to which it led. By Moses he released the Israelites, the superior race, from this bondage to the inferior, and visited his wrath upon the usurpers of his power for their unnatural and savage cruelty. He had delegated his power to Shem and Japheth to control Ham. But he never had delegated his power to Ham to rule over Shem or Japheth. The divine subordination of these races is written in the Scriptures for our learning. It is only necessary to look upon the domestic and national fields of experiment up to the present period of the world's history, to satisfy us that God's plan of subordinating individuals and races is wise, humane and good, and that the infidel theory of "freedom and equality" is only evil, and that continually.

THE END.

www.ingramcontent.com/pod-product-compliance
Lightning Source LLC
Chambersburg PA
CBHW030719110426
42739CB00030B/999